des auteurs ... j'attaque ... defaut ; ...seur un peu fâcheux, mais souvent nécessaire ...lin à blâmer que savant à bien faire ...

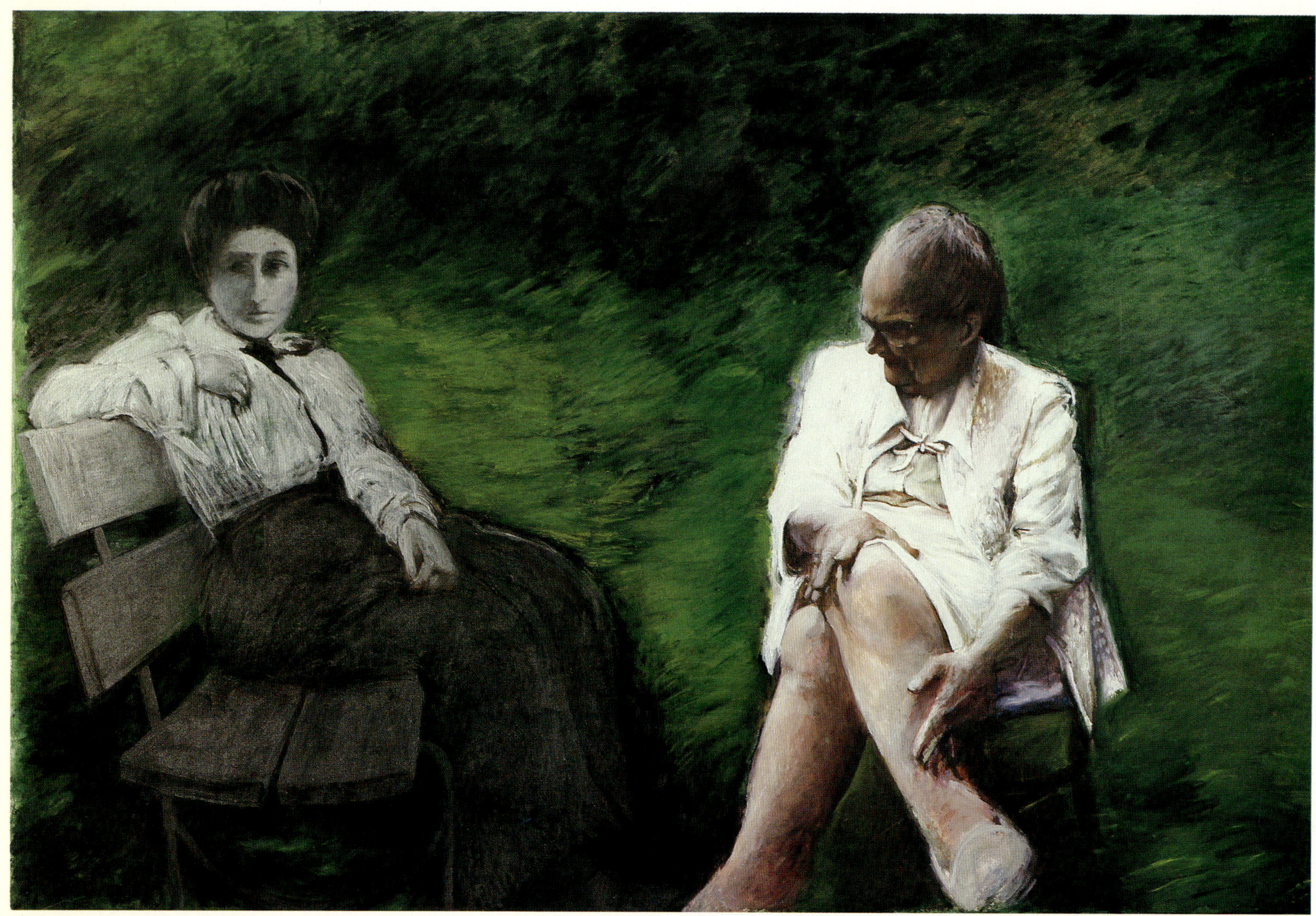

Fig. 3. *Forming the Fifth International*, 1985, acrylic/canvas, 78 × 115″, Coll. of the artist.

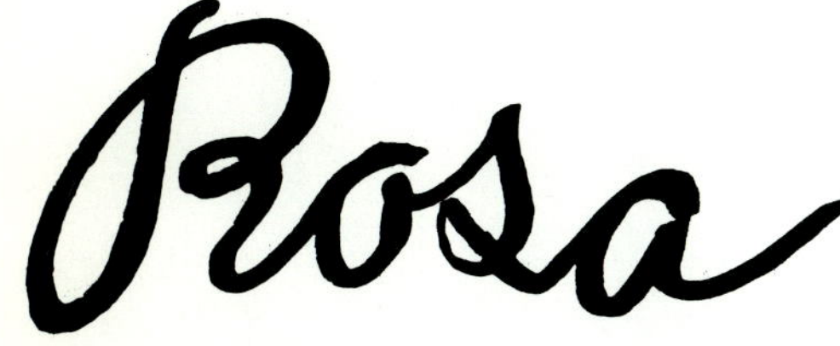

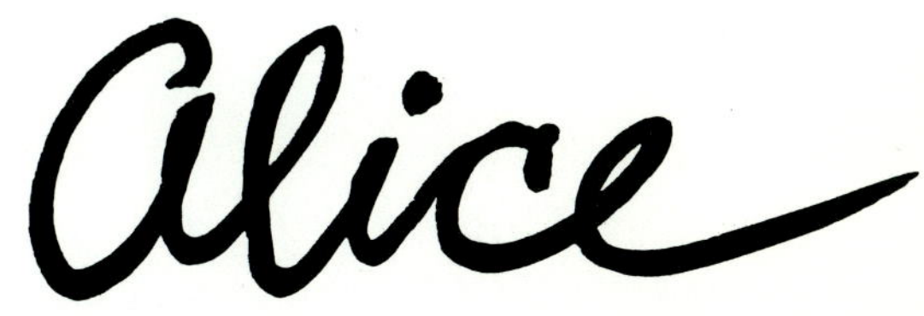

MAY STEVENS

# ORDINARY   EXTRAORDINARY

Melissa Dabakis and Janis Bell, editors

Olin Gallery • Kenyon College • Gambier, Ohio

Universe Books • New York

ISBN: 0-87663-750-0

Published in the United States of America in 1988
by Universe Books
381 Park Avenue South
New York, New York 10016





This exhibition was made possible in part by the Ohio Humanities
Council, a state-based agency of the National Endowment for the
Humanities, which makes grants to nonprofit organizations in Ohio for
public programs in the humanities.

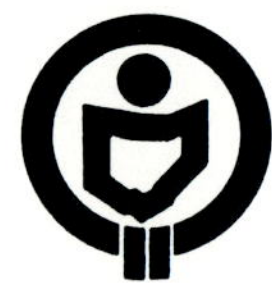

# CONTENTS

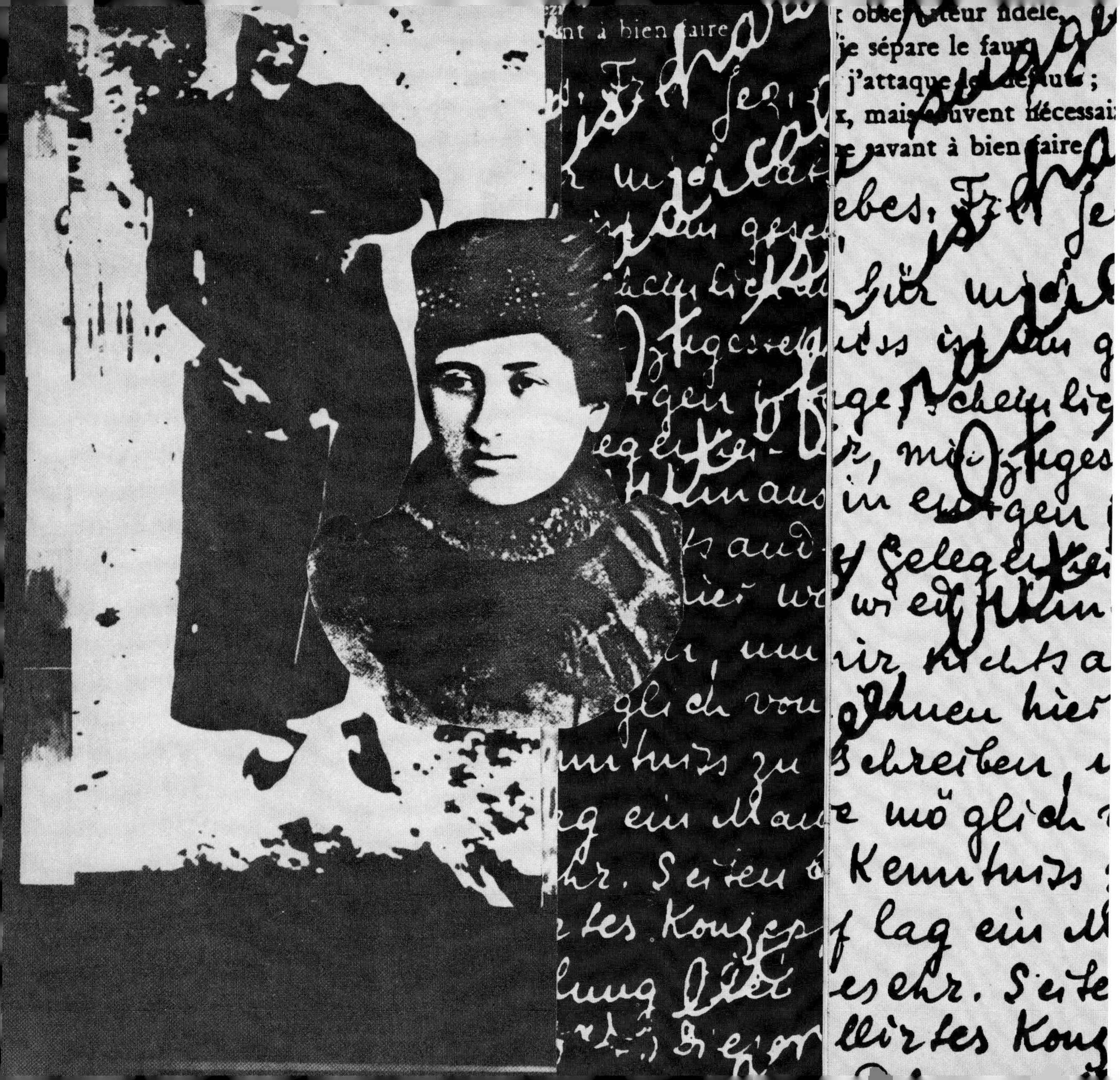

Fig. 10. *Ordinary.Extraordinary* (artist's book), 1980, detail.

# ACKNOWLEDGMENTS

Every decision about the exhibition and the catalogue has been a collaborative effort. May Stevens has guided our efforts from beginning to end, participating in the selection of works for the show and the design of the catalogue, generously supplying photographs, and carefully editing the copy for the catalogue. All of us thank her for her patience and enthusiasm, for her insightful suggestions and criticisms, and for her hospitality on our visits to her studio.

The Ohio Humanities Council generously provided funding for this catalogue and for a symposium at Kenyon College (28 February 1988) entitled "Art and Political Activism: Recent Work of May Stevens." This symposium was set up as a panel discussion with the artist, art historians Moira Roth and Patricia Mathews, historian Ellen Furlough, artist and theorist Timothy Quigley, and sociologist Howard L. Sacks. Kenyon supported the exhibition and funded several public events, including a lecture on the art of May Stevens by Moira Roth and two films by Margarethe von Trotta: *Marianne and Juliane* and *Rosa Luxemburg.* Our sincere gratitude is extended to Kenyon President Philip H. Jordan Jr., Provost Reed S. Browning, members of the Faculty Lectureships Committee, and members of the Ohio Humanities Council, who made this project possible.

Many people have worked to make this project a reality, enthusiastically contributing time and ideas. Janis Bell and Melissa Dabakis codirected the project. Claudia J. Esslinger served as artistic director, designing posters and didactic panels for the installation and contributing to the design of the catalogue. Thomas P. Stamp and Susan L. Rosenberg dedicated hours to all tasks involved in the publication of this catalogue. Barry L. Gunderson coordinated the installation of the exhibition, including a major improvement of the gallery walls. Judy Sacks energetically handled publicity for the exhibition, symposium, and other campus events. Timothy and Suzanne Quigley, Cécile Whiting, Moira Roth, and Ellen Furlough read drafts of the catalogue essay, contributing ideas and useful criticisms. Patricia Hills supplied letters and unpublished writings, provided useful ideas for developing the framework for the project, and served as a constant source of inspiration through all stages of the work. Joyce Kostenmacky Parr inspired many of us through her art and her teaching to take an active role in feminist art and activities. Howard L. Sacks and Patricia Mathews also contributed useful ideas through their participation in the symposium. We also want to thank Florence S. Lord, our department secretary; Edward F. Spodick, audiovisual coordinator; Jolinda Steiner, senior accountant; and other members of the planning and evaluation committee—Carol Mason, Donald Rice, Peter Rutkoff, and Jane A. Wemhoener—who contributed to this project in various ways.

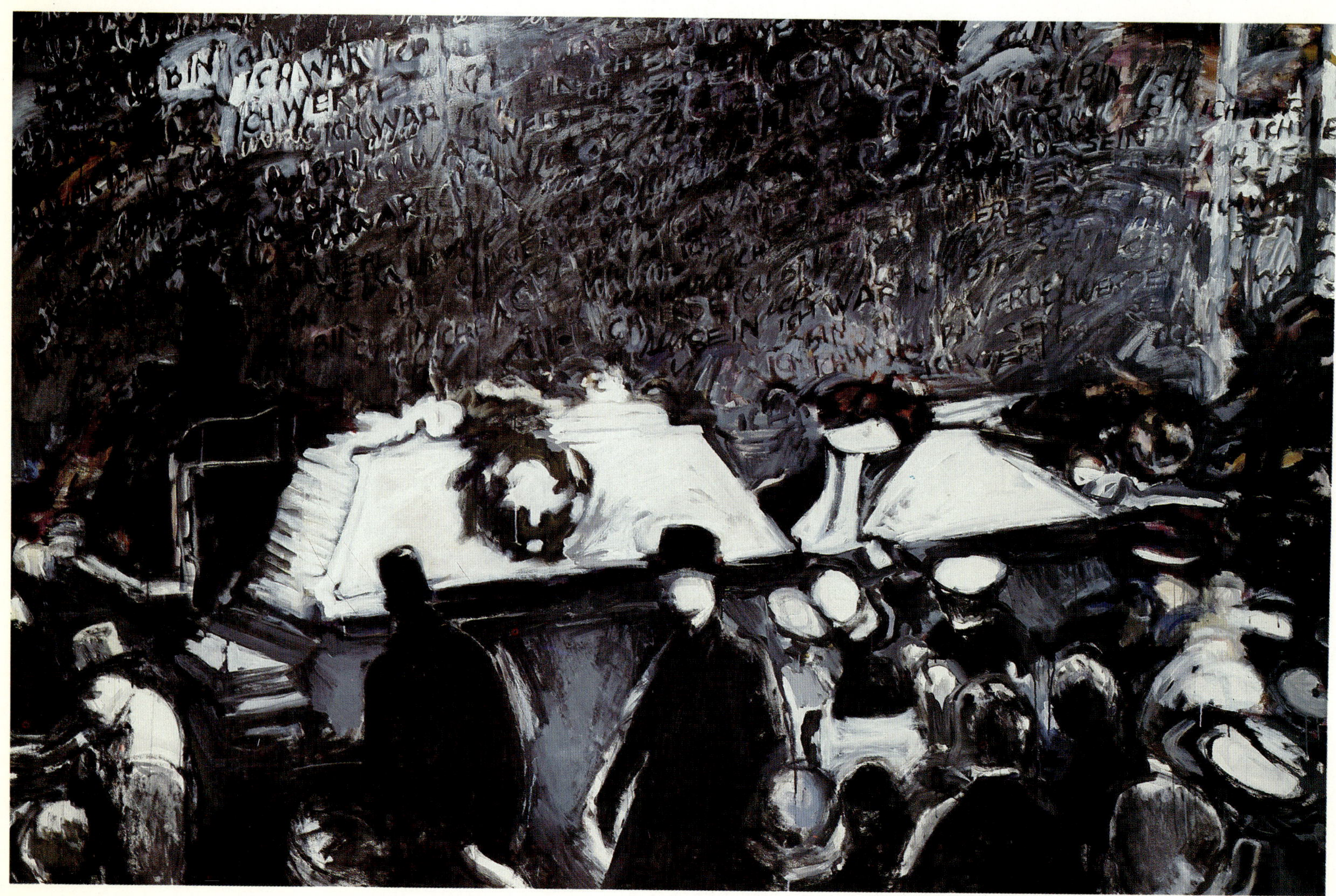

Fig. 1, *Voices*, 1983, acrylic/canvas, 79 × 118″, Coll. of the artist.

# INTRODUCTION

When the opening of the new Olin Art Gallery at Kenyon College made possible an exhibition on a larger scale than had previously been possible at Kenyon's Colburn Gallery, the suggestion of presenting the recent work of May Stevens was greeted with enthusiasm. Stevens' 1984 exhibition at Boston University, *Ordinary Extraordinary: A Summation*, was known to several faculty members of the art and art history department. Stevens' active involvement with feminism and her commitment to social and political issues suggested that an exhibition of her art would have a broad appeal, an important consideration at a small college in rural Ohio.

History is an important issue for May Stevens, and it was a crucial issue in planning a catalogue and exhibition on her work. We feel committed to the feminist cause of publishing research on women artists in order to put them into written history. This task is still as urgent now as it was in the sixties: despite the large proportion of women (38 percent) among working artists today, only a small number have works that have found their way into museums and major galleries,[1] and fewer still find their images and ideas in published catalogues and monographs. We are also committed to an approach to art history that makes known the position of women in culture, in the present and in the past.

Critics have admired the complex fabric of images that Stevens weaves from her own biography and those of her recently deceased mother, Alice Stevens, and the brilliant socialist leader of the early twentieth century, Rosa Luxemburg. She rewrites history in a way that embeds her own responses and memories within the personal and public images of her subjects. In so doing, she exposes the false dichotomy between public and private in art, history, and life. Her paintings and graphics make visible the continuing meaning of the lives of two women who had been either ignored or were soon to be forgotten. Thus, she brings what has been peripheral into focus and makes these women a paradigm for all women, "rewriting" history through images. Furthermore, her work explores issues that connect the significance of these women's lives to the continuing existence of a patriarchal society— issues of definition and categorization such as class and privilege, normal and abnormal, silent and vocal, acceptance and revolution. These issues are so seamlessly interwoven into her art and life that categorizing her as a "feminist" artist and her paintings as "feminist" art only makes evident the limitations of these categories. The richness of her individual vision does not recognize socially-imposed boundaries.

Melissa Dabakis, in her essay "Re-imagining Women's History," emphasizes the artist's connections with history—connections Stevens creates through her choice of form and content. Stevens' work makes connections to the tradition of history painting, and she values these connections for the way they create a layered texture of meaning in her works. Although they have an intrinsic emotional power as paintings, Dabakis believes that the viewer who does not know history, Rosa Luxemburg's history and May Stevens' history, or the history of feminism, will not have access to the full meaning of these works. Previous writings on works from Stevens' *Ordinary Extraordinary* series have focused on her imagery of Alice Stevens, perhaps because it was easier to see the continuity between these images and Stevens' previous *Big Daddy* series and because they made explicit the artist's feminist view that the personal is political.

Dabakis felt it was time to redress the balance by directing critical attention to the images of Rosa Luxemburg that have also occupied Stevens over the past decade and to place them within a feminist historical context. She has therefore chosen to uncover the facets of Luxemburg's life that have preoccupied Stevens, focusing on the meaning Rosa has held and still holds for the artist. Furthermore, she summarizes the chronological development of this imagery, showing how the artist has transformed a series of events in the life of one political leader into visual statements about patriarchy, gender, and class.

The exhibition *Rosa Alice* also focuses upon Luxemburg, but this should not be construed as a sign that Stevens has changed her own focus away from her mother, Alice. Quite the contrary, she continues to work with both "personalities" simultaneously, sometimes moving in divergent directions, sometimes bringing the two closer together. In choosing works for the show, Janis Bell, Melissa Dabakis, and Claudia Esslinger, together with the artist, decided to include her two most recent paintings of Alice—*Signs*, 1985 (fig. 14), and *A Life*, 1984 (fig. 2). We also decided to illustrate both in color in this catalogue, because we believe that color is a significant aspect of Stevens' work, often overlooked because of its subtlety and the difficulty of obtaining color reproductions. We are especially delighted to show—for the first time—several small photocollages.

The interview conducted by Janis Bell presents certain of the artist's ideas on her images of Alice, as well as expressing Stevens' opinions on a variety of issues related to the works in this exhibition. Stevens has published several statements and interviews in the past (see bibliography), but because these appeared before the works in this exhibition were undertaken, the interview was designed to explore the way her ideas have changed and matured and to present her ideas on other issues. Hence, the interview concentrates on working process and artistic media, on problems of dichotomies and categorization, and on formal concerns, such as color and scale in their relationship to the content of her paintings and xerographs. These passages are conversation fragments, excerpted from a two-day visit to Stevens' studio in September 1987. The interview should help to fill out our understanding of Stevens' ideas and concerns and should not be judged as a comprehensive statement of her current priorities.

"A Third Presence," a meditation by Reese Williams, was commissioned by the artist in order to present both a more spiritual point of view of her work and a "male sensitivity." Williams has been a close friend of Stevens for nearly a decade, since their involvement in the publication of her book *Ordinary Extraordinary*. Although primarily a writer and previously active in the visual arts as well, Williams recently completed training and certification as a polarity therapist. This experience expanded his awareness of physical and psychic energy. Thus, he brings an unusual sensitivity to the interpretation of Stevens' work. His essay seeks to understand her development as an artist as an outgrowth and response to significant experiences in her personal life.[2]

The catalogue also includes Stevens' "Existential Poem," written in July 1986, and reproduces *One Plus or Minus One*, her recent installation of text and photomurals at the New Museum of Contemporary Art in New York City.

Finally, the reader will find a selected bibliography, an exhibition history, and a checklist of works included in the exhibition *Rosa Alice*, held at the Olin Gallery, Kenyon College, Gambier, Ohio, February 10 through March 18, 1988.

[1]For a recent view of the problems faced by contemporary women in the art world, see Eleanor Heartney, "How Wide is the Gender Gap?" *Art News* (Summer 1987): 139-145.

[2]Williams' most recent writing is "Common Origin," in *Blasted Allegories: An Anthology of Writings by Contemporary Artists* edited by Brian Wallis (Cambridge, Massachusetts: MIT Press, 1987). Williams recently edited the anthologies *Fire over Water* (New York City: Tanam Press, 1986) and *Unwinding the Vietnam War* (Seattle, Washington: The Real Comet Press, 1987).

ROSA LUXEMBURG ON WAR: INTO THE DISILLUSIONED ATMOS-
PHERE OF PALE DAYLIGHT THERE RINGS A DIFFERENT CHORUS;
THE HOARSE CROAK OF THE HAWKS AND THE HYENAS OF THE
BATTLEFIELD. TEN THOUSAND TENTS, GUARANTEED ACCORD-
ING TO SPECIFICATIONS, 100,000 KILOS OF BACON, COCOA
POWDER, COFFEE SUBSTITUTE, CASH ON IMMEDIATE DELI-
VERY. SHRAPNEL, DRILLS, AMMUNITION BAGS, MARRIAGE
BUREAUS FOR WAR WIDOWS, LEATHER BELTS, WAR OR-
DERS — ONLY SERIOUS PROPOSITIONS CONSIDERED.
AND THE CANNON FODDER THAT WAS LOADED UPON
THE TRAINS IN AUGUST AND SEPTEMBER IS LEFT ROT-
TING ON THE BATTLEFIELDS OF BELGIUM AND THE VOSGES,
WHILE PROFITS ARE SURGING, LIKE WEEDS, FROM THE FIELDS OF DEAD.

From *The Crisis of Social Democracy*, Chapter I (New York: Socialist Publications Society, 1918).

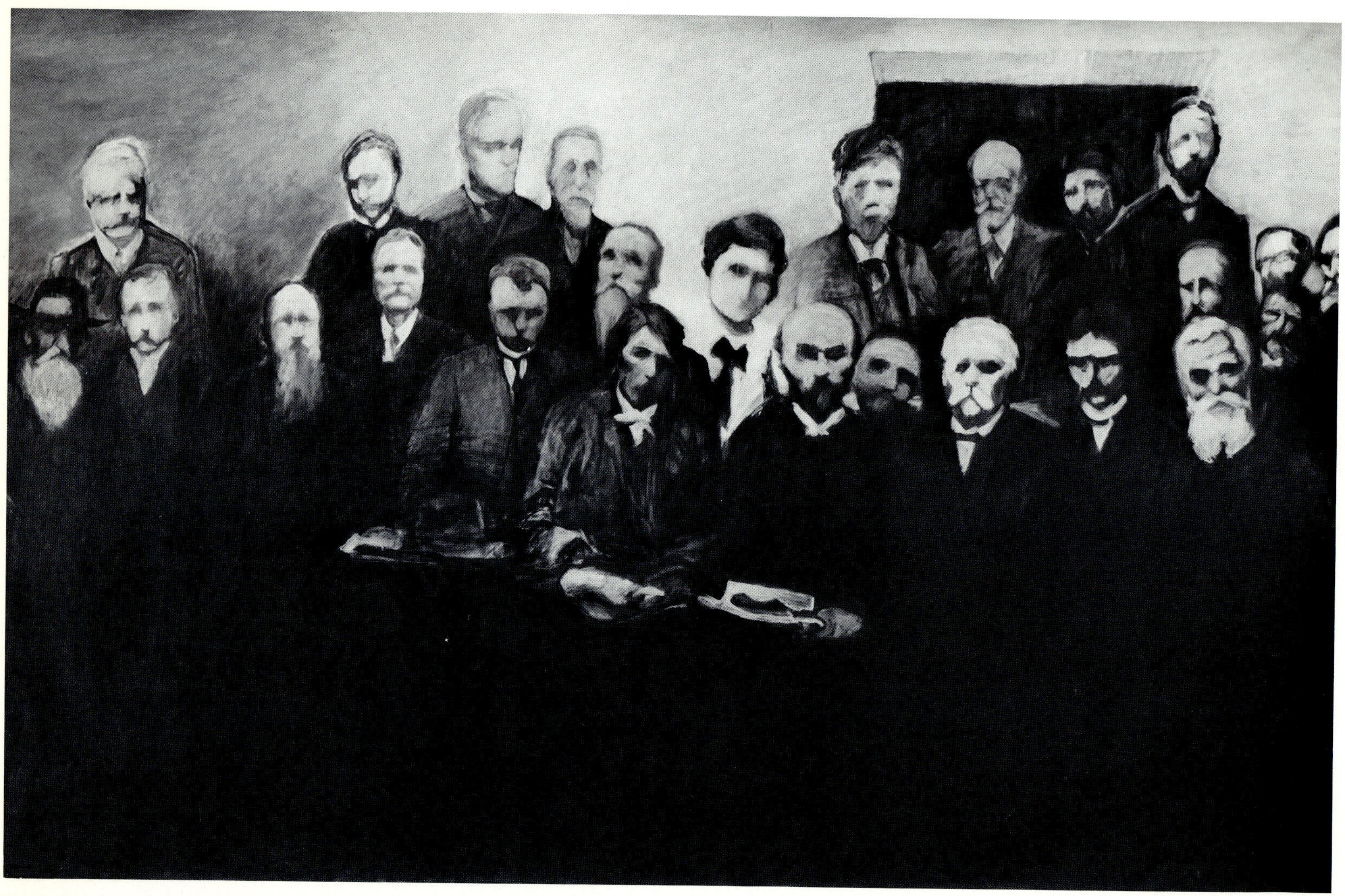

Fig. 4. *Rosa Luxemburg Attends the Second International*, 1987, acrylic/canvas, 79 × 128 ″, Coll. of the artist.

MELISSA DABAKIS

# Re-imagining WOMEN'S HISTORY

Since 1976 May Stevens *Ordinary  Extraordinary* has engaged in a dialogue with history through paintings, collages, and artist's book. Stevens has created a visual language which embodies her vision of history—a history in which women are central. In this recent series, she juxtaposes images of Alice Stevens (1895–1985), the artist's mother, with those of Rosa Luxemburg (1871–1919), the Polish/German revolutionary. She shares with other feminists working within a variety of disciplines a concern for connecting women across barriers of time, class, and culture, and has

> set up new relationships between women, vertically, in time and space, closing gaps in the generations, finding what one generation has to say to another, making knowledge cumulative, reflexive, multidimensional.[1]

This essay focuses on Rosa Luxemburg, her history, and her manifestation within the *Ordinary  Extraordinary* series. Over the past few years, Stevens has produced several new works that take Luxemburg as their theme; three of these canvases hang in the current exhibition, *Rosa  Alice*. Although a rich body of contemporary literature has analyzed the imagery of Alice Stevens and its powerful investigation into the maternal relationship, Rosa Luxemburg, a compelling mentor for the artist, has received less attention.[2] This essay addresses this critical omission by illustrating those aspects of Luxemburg's life which have particular significance to Stevens and by grounding her treatment

of Luxemburg within an historical and political context. The complex visual imagery shared by the artist's book, collages, and paintings metaphorically connects the lives of Rosa Luxemburg and Alice Stevens, whose imaginary relationship is layered with personal and political meaning.

The *Ordinary  Extraordinary* series revisualizes women's history by collapsing the traditional categories of public and private and suggesting in visual terms the feminist credo that "the personal is the political." In images and words, Stevens provides a compelling vision of the lives of these two women. Presenting both the public and private Rosa and refuting a hierarchical distinction between these two spheres of activity, Stevens shows us the powerful socialist fighter who infused her revolutionary goals with a tender and humane spirit. In depicting Alice, Stevens makes public and monumental the marginal life of a working-class woman. Her personal world of silent suffering comes to represent the political oppression of all disadvantaged women. "I think there are some people who don't want to look at this woman," Stevens has remarked. "They don't think she should be in art; in fact, they don't think she should be anywhere."[3]

For Stevens, history is a living and dynamic force, functioning dialectically with the present. As historians have argued, contemporary attitudes and beliefs inform our analysis of the past, and our understanding of history affects our actions in the present.[4] This complex dialogue between past and present forms the basis for Stevens' treatment of Rosa and Alice. Likewise, feminist historians have suggested that without linking the personal and the historical, the possibility of individual or collective action is inconceivable.

Without knowledge of historical roots, our view of daily life remains at the level of individual reaction to what strikes us as intolerable. Our analyses tend to document our feelings of subjection rather than the underlying conditions of the subjection of all women. Through *historical* studies of women, as changing diversified participants in social development, we can begin to answer the question, on what basis do women share an historical existence?[5]

The circumstances that informed the oppression of Alice Stevens' life—class and patriarchy—were in part governed by specific historical events. Rosa Luxemburg, an historical personage who attempted to alter those very circumstances that oppressed the life of Alice Stevens, fought for socialism with the hope that it would create an ideal democratic world. Stevens' art brings the legacy of Rosa Luxemburg before us, as in the painting *Voices*, 1983 (fig. 1), and reinstates the life of Alice Stevens in such works as *A Life*, 1984 (fig. 2), making their lives resonate in our contemporary world.

Rosa Luxemburg captured Stevens' imagination both for her political power and for the personal contradictions inherent in her life. Born in Zamosc, Poland, on March 5, 1871, Rosa, the youngest of five children, was raised in a Jewish though partially assimilated family. When she was three, the family moved to Warsaw, where she was treated for a congenital hip dislocation that kept her confined to bed for a year; the illness left her with an incurable limp. A talented high school student, she was accepted to the University of Zurich in 1889 (one of the few universities to grant admission to women at the time) where she received her doctorate in economics. In Zurich, as part of an exhilarating international socialist community, she committed herself to a life of political activism.

Strident, forceful, and at times abrasive, Luxemburg has been hailed as one of the most original socialist thinkers of the twentieth century.

Her life represents an heroic struggle against militarism, nationalism, and imperialism. "There are few monuments to the socialist pursuit of freedom, but the life of Rosa Luxemburg is surely one of them," writes historian Stephen Eric Bronner.[6] However, her relationship to the questions of feminism, anti-Semitism, and racism remains ambiguous. For Luxemburg, the proletarian revolution demanded her life's effort, thus her focused pursuit of a classless society blinded her to the exigencies of related political issues. She idealistically believed that the oppression of women, Jews, and people of color would come to an end with the creation of a just socialist society. It was exactly this complexity and contradiction within her character that drew Stevens to Rosa Luxemburg and which the *Ordinary Extraordinary* series captures and shares.

In her theoretical writings, Luxemburg constructed a model for socialism that is as yet untried. She attained prominence in the respected German Socialist Party as early as 1899 by defending orthodox Marxist socialism against revisionism. She was the only woman to rise to prominence in the Second International, becoming an ally yet a perceptive critic of V.I. Lenin.[7] She repeatedly challenged Lenin's advocacy of an elite vanguard party composed of a small number of dedicated intellectuals who would inject revolutionary consciousness into the workers. Acting along principles of "democratic centralism," the party, to Lenin, incarnated the true class interests of the workers.[8] Luxemburg saw this as authoritarianism and deadening to the process of revolution. Unlike Lenin, who relied upon a strict party structure, Luxemburg held an unyielding faith in the working classes and their ability for self-administration. She argued that the interests of the party were not identical with those of the working class and believed, in fact, that the party should be led by the masses.[9] Although a strong supporter of the Russian Revolution, she feared the outcome of Lenin's authoritarianism in her writing of 1917:

> Socialism in life demands a complete spiritual transformation in the masses degraded by centuries of bourgeois class rule . . ..
> No one knows this better than Lenin. But he is completely mistaken in the means he employs. Decree, dictatorial force of the factory overseer, Draconian penalties, rule by terror—all these

things are but palliatives. The only way to rebirth is the school of public life itself, the most unlimited, the broadest democracy and public opinion. It is the rule by terror that demoralizes . . ..

Without general elections, without a free struggle of opinion, life dies out in every public institution, becomes a mere semblance of life, in which only the bureaucracy remains as the active element . . .. at bottom, then, a clique affair—a dictatorship of the proletariat, however, but only the dictatorship of a handful of politicians, that is a dictatorship in the bourgeois sense . . .[10]

Although adamant in her criticism of the Bolshevik model, Luxemburg would come to appreciate the need for a strong party organization in 1919 when she and Karl Liebknecht would lead an unsuccessful attempt at social revolution in Germany.

Luxemburg hoped to forge a unity between spontaneity and organization which would allow the political maturity of the working class to develop.[11] The mass strike was her preferred weapon for revolutionary change. Originating with the workers, the revolution would take its direction from the spontaneous actions of its members.[12] In encouraging the workers to control their own destinies, she developed a unique position in the history of socialist thought and provided an alternative to the revolutionary plan defined by Lenin and later enforced to extremes by Joseph Stalin.

During the years 1905 to 1909, Luxemburg reached her height of influence in the German Social Democratic Party. But by 1910 her commitment to social revolution caused a bitter split with the conservative elements of the party. To Luxemburg revolution had living potential; to the Social Democratic Party it had only theoretical relevance. By the end of her life, she had incurred the wrath of the Social Democrats who had compromised their vision through acquiescence to the military and capitulation to established authority. In 1919, it was the German Social Democratic Party that turned its back on Luxemburg and consented to her murder.

The vigor with which Luxemburg pursued the revolution has become her hallmark in historical literature. In her most noted work, the *Accumulation of Capital* of 1913, a critique of capitalism based on the

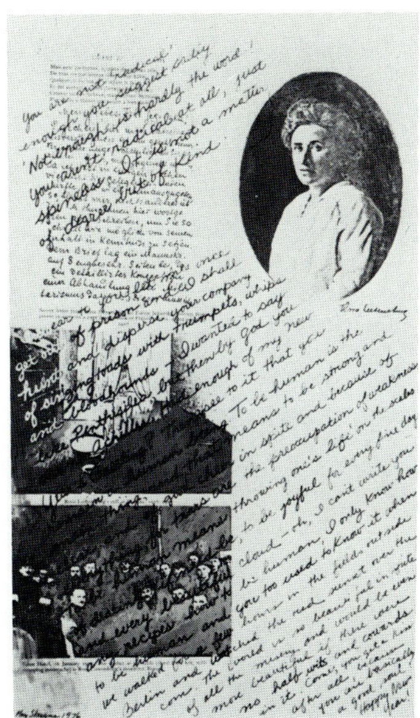

Fig. 6. *Tribute to Rosa Luxemburg*, 1976, mixed-media collage, 16.5 × 10″, Coll: Rudolf Baranik.

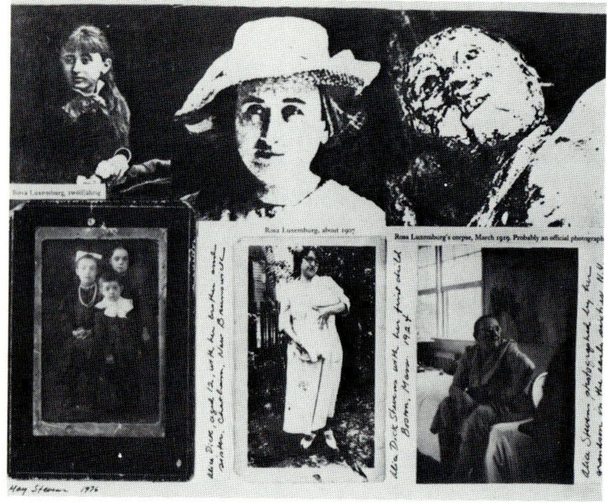

Fig. 5. *Two Women*, 1976, mixed-media collage, 10.5 × 13.5 ", Coll: Rudolf Baranik.

writings of Marx, she argued that capitalism is an international system intrinsically linked to imperialism, refuting the commonly-held perception that imperialism marked only one stage of capitalism.[13] Her revolutionary fervor, even joy, continues to astound.

> The period when I was writing *Accumulation* belongs to the happiest in my life. I really lived as if in a state of intoxication, day and night seeing nothing but this one problem that was unfolding itself so beautifully in front of me, and I don't know which afforded me greater pleasure: the thinking process, whereby I pondered a complicated question while slowly walking up and down the room . . . or the shaping of results into literary form on paper. Do you know I wrote the entire 30 galleys in one go within 4 months—something unheard of!—and that I sent off the rough draft to the printer without even once reading it over?[14]

As brilliant and fluent as Luxemburg's words were, she never failed to assess their effectiveness with a sharp criticality. In describing the *Anti-Critique*, an addendum to her book, she wrote to a friend:

> Naturally, the reader must, in order to appreciate my *Anti-Critique*, be a master of national economy in general and Marxism in particular, and that to the nth degree. And how many such mortals are there today? Not a half-dozen. My work is from this standpoint truly a luxury product and might just as well be printed on handmade paper.[15]

Her sensitivity to the complexity of political action is apparent in her words. Always wishing to keep in touch with the workers, she was fully aware that such profound theoretical writing spoke only to the educated and the privileged. For that reason, she cast her speeches and writings in the popular press in a language that made them the most influential and accessible socialist propaganda of the time.

Luxemburg was imprisoned during the years 1915–1918 for her outspoken opposition to the pro-war policies of Kaiser Wilhelm, which the German Social Democratic Party supported. From her prison cell, she continued her political writing and upheld the founding of the Spartacist League, a radical splinter group of the Social Democratic Party. Upon her release, she joined Liebknecht, also jailed for his antimilitarist views, to assume leadership of a revolution under way in the streets of Berlin. With the defeat of Germany in World War I and the abdication of the Kaiser, mass strikes had broken out throughout Germany. At first, Luxemburg was exhilarated by the outburst of revolutionary fervor demonstrated by the masses, but quickly she realized that the revolution had no organizational base. After much debate among political factions, she helped found the Communist Party of Germany, a fledgling organization too weak to guide the revolutionary energies. With no strong direction, the mass uprisings were eventually quelled by the German military.

Hunted by the soldiers of the Weimar Government, a coalition of German Democratic Socialists and the military of the old order, Luxemburg dispatched a scathing critique of the German state for the Communist paper, *Die Rote Fahne*, shortly before her capture.

> "Order reigns in Warsaw!"—"Order reigns in Paris!"—"Order reigns in Berlin!" And so run the reports of the guardians of "order" every half-century, from one center of the world-historical struggle to another. And the rejoicing "victors" do not notice that an "order" which must be periodically maintained by bloody butchery is steadily approaching its historical destiny, its doom. The revolution will "raise itself up again clashing," and to your horror it will proclaim to the sound of trumpets: *I was, I am, I shall be.*[16]

On January 5, 1919, Luxemburg and Liebknecht were killed by German soldiers, with the tacit consent of the German Socialist Party leaders Friedrich Ebert and Gustav Noske. Liebknecht was taken away first and shot—ostensibly when he attempted to escape.[17] Luxemburg was captured later, fully expecting to be returned to prison. Instead, she was bludgeoned with the butt of a rifle, then shot in the head. Her body was thrown into the Landwehr Canal and retrieved five months later.

Huge parades of mourners paid their respects to these influential socialist leaders. Artists and writers alike kept their memory alive. Mies van der Rohe erected the *Monument to Karl Liebknecht and other Spartacists* in Friedrichsfelde Cemetery, Berlin, in 1926 (it was later destroyed by the Nazis in 1933).[18] Kathe Kollwitz, Max Beckmann, George Grosz,

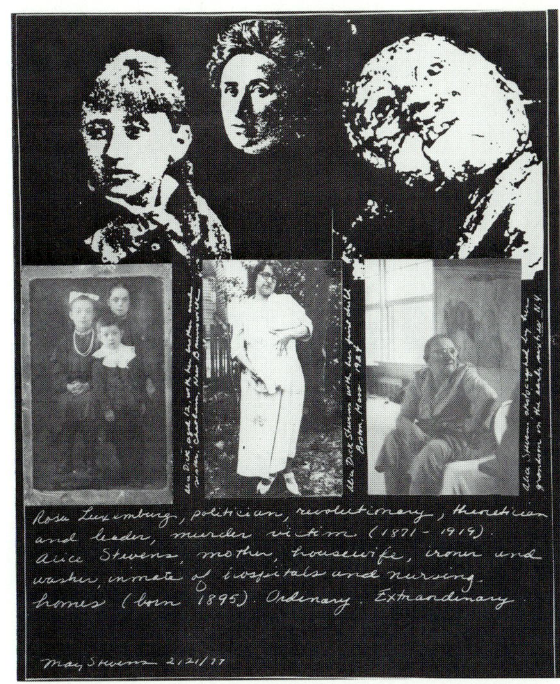


Fig. 7. *Rosa and Alice*, 1977, mixed-media collage, 22 × 17", Coll: Patricia Hills.

and most recently R.B. Kitaj and Stevens have dedicated work to these revolutionaries.[19] Criticized for her stance on issues of gender and race, Luxemburg had been the center of critical debate among historians of women. It is only recently that her life has been reconsidered by feminist historians, filmmakers, and artists, as evidenced by Elzbieta Ettinger's biography *Rosa Luxemburg: A Life* and Margarethe von Trotta's film *Rosa Luxemburg*, both of 1986.

Considered a "reluctant feminist" by many historians, Luxemburg perceived feminist concerns as secondary to the more central issue of class struggle. She never identified herself fully with the "women's question" for fear of being relegated to the periphery of political activity. As an exceptional woman who broke from a traditional feminine role, Luxemburg fell under the influence of the prevailing masculine ideology which considered "women's work" (including feminist concerns) outside the sphere of important political activity. Considered an equal (or superior) to most of the male party leadership, Luxemburg nonetheless responded to issues of her own gender and at times openly supported women's emancipation. In 1898 she met Clara Zetkin, the leader of the German Women's Movement, with whom she became lifelong friends. Supporting the first International Women's Day in 1911, she wrote to her friend Luise Kautsky, "Are you coming for the women's conference? Just imagine, I have become a feminist! I received a credential for this [first International Women's Suffrage] conference and must therefore go to Jena."[20] By 1912, she was writing essays for *Die Gleichheit*, the Social Democratic Women's Journal which Zetkin edited for nearly twenty-five years. Among those articles published were "Women's Voting Rights and the Class Struggle" and "The Proletarian Woman."[21]

For Luxemburg as for Zetkin, the issue of class was inseparable from that of gender. In fact, both understood women's emancipation in terms of a working-class mass movement.[22] Luxemburg wrote in "Women's Voting Rights and the Class Struggle:"

> Today, it is the proletarian woman's turn to make the capitalist state conscious of her maturity. This is done through a constant, powerful mass movement which has to use all the means of proletarian struggle and pressure.
>
> Women's suffrage is the goal. But the mass movement to bring it about is not a job for women alone, but it is a common class concern for women and men of the proletariat.

She bitterly harangued bourgeois women whom she saw as being as much the enemy of socialism as the men in power. She continued:

> Aside from the few who have jobs or professions, the women of the bourgeoisie do not take part in social production. They are nothing but co-consumers of the surplus value their men extort from the proletariat. They are parasites of the parasites of the social body. And co-consumers are usually even more rabid and cruel in defending their "right" to a parasite's life than the direct agent of class rule and exploitation.[23]

In her opposition to the war, Luxemburg worked closely with working-class women's groups and grew increasingly supportive of feminist issues. Not only did she see women as strong allies in her antimilitarist campaign, but she began to understand that women were fighting their inferior status and powerlessness to determine their own lives and those of their children. In 1915, Luxemburg planned to participate in the International Women's Conference in Bern, but she was jailed before she had the opportunity to attend.[24] To be sure, feminism and the proletarian revolution were never fully reconciled in her short and brutally-ended life. But her life serves as a model of women's liberation; she was an active political force in a world dominated by men. Against great odds, she achieved respect from her male counterparts as a brilliant theoretician, speaker, and political strategist. Indeed, her life offered a vivid example of the expanded definition of "womanhood" itself.

Although rising to prominence in the patriarchal world of socialist politics, Luxemburg never denied her womanhood, her personal life, or her humanity. She conceived of social revolution in a strikingly new manner, envisioning a process of revolution that retained its humanity by seeking no distinction between a personal need for happiness and the joy and contentment of the masses. As a revolutionary leader, she sought to infuse the political goal of liberation with an acknowledgment of the personal and the human. She wrote from her prison cell in

Wronke on 28 December 1916:

> See to it that you remain a *human being*. To be human is the main
> thing, and that means to be strong and clear and of *good cheer* in
> spite and because of everything, for tears are the preoccupation of
> weakness. To be human means throwing one's life on the scales of
> destiny, if need be, to be joyful for every fine day and every beauti-
> ful cloud—oh, I can't write you any recipes how to be human, I
> only know how to be human . . . .[25]

She brought the personal force of her spirit to politics and created a new
model for the political activist, rejecting the traditional image of the
revolutionary as defined by Sigmund Freud and evidenced by political
leaders such as Lenin.[26] It was exactly that definition characterized by
the Russian anarchists M.A. Bakunin and S.G. Nechaev that Rosa
abhorred:

> The revolutionary is a lost man; he has no interests of his own, no
> cause of his own, no feelings, no habits, no belongings; he does
> not have even a name. Everything in him is absorbed by a single,
> exclusive interest, a single thought, a single passion—the revolu-
> tion . . .. All the tender feelings of family life, of friendship, love,
> gratitude, and even honor must be stifled in him by a single cold
> passion—the revolutionary cause.[27]

Yet the man she adored, Leo Jogiches, with whom love and politics
commingled, embodied this image. Rosa struggled with this contradiction. She urged him to fulfill her ideal—always wanting more intimacy
but never receiving it. She wrote to him on 6 March 1899:

> I felt happiest about the part of your letter in which you wrote that
> we are both still young and able to arrange our personal life. Oh,
> Dyodyo, my golden one, if only you keep your promise! . . . Our
> own small apartment, our own nice furniture, our own library,
> quiet and regular work, walks together, an opera from time to
> time, small, *very* small, circle of friends who can sometimes be
> invited for dinner; every year a summer vacation in the country,
> one month with absolutely no work! . . . And perhaps even a
> little, a very little baby? . . . We will *both* work and life will be
> *perfect*!! No couple on earth has the chance we have. With just a

little goodwill we will be happy, we must.[28]

She perceived that socialism had to be made from the inside out—that
the ideals and values of the new society rested in the hearts of leaders
and masses alike. This was the "spiritual transformation" of society
about which she argued with Lenin. She wanted to make a socialist
home with Jogiches, to keep alive the promise of this new social vision.[29]

Rosa Luxemburg was not afraid to love. Her letters to Jogiches were
filled with warm loving messages, but from her lover she received letters
principally devoted to political concerns. In a letter of 1900, she replied,
"When I open your letters and see six sheets covered with debates about
the Polish Socialist Party and not a single word about . . . ordinary life, I
feel faint."[30] Painfully disappointing to Rosa, the promise of their relationship was never fulfilled.

Luxemburg's single most important contribution to feminist thinking concerned the humanization of her political struggle. Feminist
historians have recently emphasized this point in their work, collapsing
the traditionally separate spheres of personal and political.[31] Recon-
sidering the view of history defined by power, political influence, and
visibility—spheres of activity from which women have traditionally
been excluded—feminist historians have brought a new understanding
to the practice of history.

> We are learning that the writing of women into history necessarily
> involves redefining and enlarging traditional notions of historical
> significance, to encompass personal, subjective experience as well
> as public and political activities. It is not too much to suggest that
> however hesitant the actual beginnings, such a methodology
> implies not only a new history of women, but also a new history.[32]

In recent writing, feminist authors have begun to synthesize the
public and private aspects of Luxemburg's life. In contrast to traditional
biographers, who have tended to define history as the political activities
of great men, feminists and other contemporary writers have ques-
tioned this definition of power and have sought to integrate the personal
and the political into historical discourse. Elzbieta Ettinger, the author
of the recent Luxemburg biography, argues that revealing the personal
life of a historical personage was not enough; it was necessary to show

the full person replete with weaknesses and struggles. She explains:

> The revolutionary who emerged in the pages [of *Letters from Prison*, published in 1920] was a spiritual giant and a lyrical dreamer. She possessed an almost supernatural inner strength, was immune to ordinary personal tribulations and anxieties, loved humanity, animals, birds, and flowers . . .. the letters created and perpetuated a myth.

In her biography, Ettinger presents material on Luxemburg from the Zwickau letters as well, which "reveal the real person—plagued with doubts about herself, about her lover, about life."[33]

On the other hand James Joll, the prominent historian of the Second International, criticizes Ettinger for this stance. In a recent review he wrote, ". . . it is both pathetic and ironic to see the famous Marxist revolutionary writing to her love, 'I've two vases with violets on the table and a pink lampshade . . . and new gloves, and a new hairbrush and I'm pretty.' "[34] Exactly that which demystified the awe-inspiring revolutionary, which brought her closer to our personal lives, Joll wishes to banish from the writing of history. That which made the past live, which made it relevant to our contemporary situation, has been systematically excluded from a traditional definition of history.

Stevens' commitment to history, feminism, and socialism drew her to the life of Rosa Luxemburg. In *Forming the Fifth International*, 1985 (fig. 3), and *Rosa Luxemburg Attends the Second International*, 1987 (fig. 4), she enters into dialogue with Rosa, and through her art invites us to engage with history. Stevens explains:

> [Rosa's] myth makes it impossible to identify with her, which is one of the reasons for looking at her more closely and more complexly . . . .. As feminists, we should never be awestruck . . . by Rosa because what that does is prevent us from being Rosa or doing Rosa. What we should say about Rosa is that this is a real flesh and blood woman, who lived and was talented and had some breaks given, made others happen . . ."[35]

Through painting on a monumental scale and such alternative media as collages and her artist's book, Stevens revitalizes historical content, re-imagining the life of Rosa Luxemburg and making it relevant to con-

temporary political concerns. As Alan Wallach explains,

> in rejecting traditional history painting, the [nineteenth-century] avant garde, for the most part, rejected history, or rather saw a choice between the personal and the historical, and opted for the personal. In the twentieth century, the rejection of the historical hardened into dogma . . .. How much still might be gained from a synthesis of the personal and the historical is suggested by the work of a number of contemporary artists [Stevens among them].[36]

Stevens instills the lived experience in her notion of history. Her paintings, while sharing her respect for the past, also present a private intuitive moment of reflection. For Stevens,

> the historical content of these paintings involves an expressionism that re-experiences what was never before experienced. Not documentation but a shadow thrown up from historical origins, its power consists in the distance it has come.[37]

Through evocation and imagination, Stevens reinterprets the past. Her art enters and impresses upon the public sphere of history.

In developing the *Ordinary Extraordinary* series, Stevens made multimedia collages and her artist's book before turning to large paintings.[38] Two collages, entitled *Two Women*, 1976 (fig. 5), and *Tribute to Rosa Luxemburg*, 1976 (fig. 6), which would become the opening pieces in this series, were reproduced in the first issue of *Heresies: A Feminist Publication on Art and Politics*. Stevens helped found this journal in 1976 and still serves as an associate member of the *Heresies* collective. These collages, comprising photocopies of photographs articulated into complex and unexpected juxtapositions, are infinitely reproducible works of art. They defy the notion of a priceless commodity or of a precious artwork.[39] They are small-scale and intimate, made to be handled and closely scrutinized. Like a family album, they invite participation and suggest the complex and subtle relationships that women share through time and history. As Lisa Tickner writes:

> Elements from different modes of experience, different systems of meaning (family albums, Edwardian dresses, political pamphlets, private letters, remembered speech, police photographs)— emotionally charged and dense with their original reference—are

overwritten and overlaid, "pieced," to use a female metaphor, in new patterns of association and contiguity: imbricated and inter-leaved. Like much feminist work it attempts to . . . incorporate into the area of legitimate cultural expression a range of tradition-ally silent positions and speakers; and to assert the interdepen-dence of the conventionally opposed—the public and the private, politics and autobiography.[40]

In *Two Women*, Stevens creates an interplay between Rosa and Alice through visual interconnections and thematic overlays. Both women are presented with a chronology of their lives: at age twelve, at maturity, and at death and dying. As children, the two women share the same wide-eyed innocence, yet in subsequent photographs, it is clear that Alice—holding her first-born (the artist) tenderly, awkwardly, and tentatively—is entrapped in a domestic sphere that would ultimately suffocate her. As the artist recounts,

> My mother, when I was growing up, did not sew, did not cook well, and did not keep a beautiful house. She had been forced to leave elementary school when her father died. She had no social graces and no talents. She only loved me and my brother without question. When my brother died at sixteen and I left home, the long disorientation consumed her and she was committed to a state mental hospital.

> Sexism and classicism, male authority and poverty-and-ignorance were the forces that crippled my mother; the agent in most direct contact with her was, of course, my father. But the equation cannot be written as two equal forces of sex and class focusing their oppressive powers through one man onto my mother. Poverty (class) ground her down from the beginning (when it took a bright child out of school to make her a mother's helper to the rich folk on the hill) and used male dominance to do it (her brother was kept in school) and religion to sanctify the arrangement and squelch her own desire. She was taught to be good. She was a good student. She was always good—until she painted the kitchen red in the middle of the night and screamed at passing cars.[41]

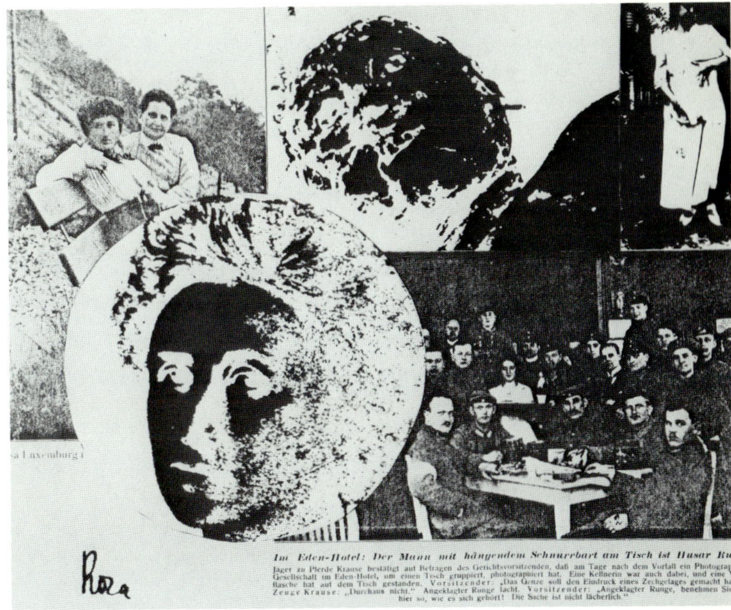

Fig. 8. *Roza*, 1980, mixed-media collage , 42 × 52 ", Coll. of the artist.

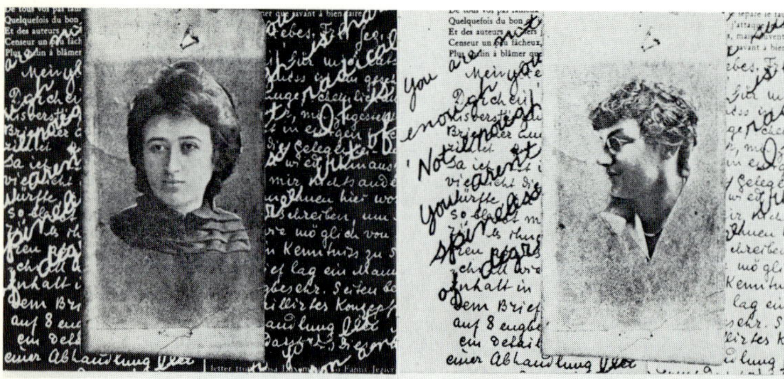

Fig. 9. *Ordinary.Extraordinary* (artist's book), 1980.

This image of Alice is juxtaposed to Rosa, who in 1907, the date of the photograph, was at her height of power in the Social Democratic Party. Elegantly dressed, a privileged middle-class upbringing clearly apparent, she addressed the world with confidence and vigor. A pivotal year in her life, she broke her intimate relationship with Jogiches and as a result developed her own theoretical independence.[42] But at the same time, Rosa would have envied Alice her children and their love—an intimate need never fulfilled.

These four images, iconically frontal, are distinct from the image of Rosa's bloated corpse, pulled from the river several months after her murder, and that of the elderly Alice, institutionalized since the early 1950s, seated before a window. They form a diagonal, moving directly out into the viewer's space. They speak of death—of the injustice of lives cut short. Stevens writes: "When [Alice] read the newspaper she said: Some people died who never died before. They died just now, she said."[43] In another version of this collage, *Rosa and Alice*, 1977 (fig. 7)[44] the figure of Alice and the background consist of pieced photographs. Alice's world was not whole but fragmented and disjunctive; although alive, she withdrew from the physical world into a separate, private sphere. Alice, it seemed, had died before.

In *Tribute to Rosa Luxemburg*, it is the revolutionary to whom Stevens pays homage. Overlaid with excerpts of Rosa's private writings are images associated with her imprisonment and murder. Stevens appropriates three photographs: a 1917 prison letter from Rosa, secretly written in urine on a page of poetry; her cell in Wronke, which as a political prisoner she was allowed to furnish with her own belongings; and members of the Freikorps guard who celebrated after murdering her. The historical references are not arbitrary, but described by the captions that accompany each photograph. Rosa's words speak clearly as Stevens restates her letter: "See to it that you remain a human being . . . " The image of Rosa, unobscured by layerings of print, is enframed within an oval, the conventional format for the photographic image that served as Stevens' artistic source. Nonetheless, within this constructed collage, this motif is reminiscent of a sacred mandorla. Thus, Stevens imaginatively reconstructs Rosa's story—using the conventions of Western art in creating a modern myth and/or history for women.

In later collages, such as *Roza*, 1980 (fig. 7), Stevens begins to work on a larger scale (42″ × 52″), no longer inviting the same intimate interaction between image and viewer. Motifs are used and reused: Rosa in life and death. A photographic negative of her portrait is encircled and set against a negative image of the head of her corpse. In positive forms Rosa, seated in a landscape with Luise Kautsky, is opposed to an image of death, the murderer's celebration. Overlooking the scene in the upper right corner is Alice holding May, witnesses to history and heirs to Rosa's struggle.

In 1980, Stevens received a grant to publish her *Ordinary Extraordinary* artist's book. In keeping with the spirit of the first collages, Stevens produced a format in which the viewer (reader) could actively participate.[45] In the book, the verbal and visual texts readapt those used in many of the collages, although several new images and writings also appear. Stevens explains:

> [The page-size collages] were gathered into the artist's book which naturally meant changes in them, additions and subtractions, the creation of new images as well. For the book I was extremely concerned with continuity, flow-through. In my concept front and back cover had to wrap around the book. Turning the pages was/is a journey of one thing leading into another with the pacing controlled by the material on each page.[46]

Stevens uses the technique of overlay not only with the written word but also with visual images. On the fourth and fifth page of the book, reproductions of old photographs of Rosa and Alice as young women are juxtaposed (fig. 8). Over layers of written text in French, German, and English are photos, themselves overlays, suggesting that Alice resided beneath Rosa and Rosa beneath Alice. The images of these two women exist as pentimenti for each other. In these collages, history as filtered through consciousness is suggested yet never totally decipherable. "Consciousness operates on many levels," Stevens notes,

> the past stretches back to preconsciousness, punctuated by images and voices that never totally leave us; our minds slip from

memory to desire without a seam . . .[47]
Stevens' paintings and collages resonate with layers of meaning. They simulate our experience of consciousness, bringing memory and imagination together as one. They embody an intuitive dimension that informs our relationship to the world and our understanding of history.

On the following page, the same text in three languages makes a total ground (fig. 10). Overlaid are images of the young Rosa and Alice holding her child—a negative of Alice in such high contrast as to eliminate detail and abstract her form. The presence of the child is subsumed within the black silhouette of Alice; however, between Rosa and Alice, a bold white shape appears, suggesting a uterus and birth canal, an abstract shape connecting Alice, Rosa, and May. The bonding of womanhood and the symbolism of mother—both natural and adopted—come together to shape this image.

In 1981, Stevens began to paint these images on a large scale. But unlike the mixed-media collages and book, the paintings maintain separate spheres for Alice and Rosa, each acting individually upon a distinct ground. Her first large-scale painting (78″ × 142″), *Everybody Knows Me*, 1981 (fig. 11), translated into acrylic on canvas the images of Alice from the *Two Women* collage. Replicating the high-contrast effect of the photocopying process, Stevens created an interplay both formally and iconographically with the collages and book, breaking down the traditional barriers between high art (painting) and popular media (photography, photocopy). Moreover, Stevens used the processed image as a metaphor for memory, re-presenting the tracings and markings of lived experience.

In this triptych-like format, Stevens articulated a progression through time and space. The image of the young Alice with her siblings is placed highest on the canvas suggesting the greatest distance in space and time. In contrast, the image of the elderly Alice occupies the entire frame, her figure, diagonally situated, pressed close to the picture plane, and in immediate contact with the viewer. Working on such a monumental scale, Stevens evoked the tradition of history painting as redefined by Gustave Courbet—the humble and the ordinary as significant content for artistic expression. Alice is at once the unique individual and every aged working-class woman, just as Courbet's peasant grandfather becomes the focus of ritual and ceremony in his *Burial at Ornans*.[48]

Continuing to work on paintings of Alice Stevens over the next several years—*Fore River*, 1983 (fig. 12), *Go Gentle*, 1983 (fig. 13), *A Life*, 1984 (fig. 2), and *Signs*, 1985 (fig. 14)—Stevens also paid tribute to Luxemburg in other works. In *Dreams and Theories I*, 1981 (fig. 15), and *Dreams and Theories II*, 1981 (fig. 16), she presents the private Rosa, seated outdoors in conversation with Luise Kautsky. *Dreams and Theories II* is inspired by a photograph used in the collage *Roza* of the previous year. *Dreams and Theories I* presents a variation of this motif where the figures are viewed from the back. In this image Rosa turns, her arm draped over the bench back, and addresses the viewer directly. The forms of the figures are modeled with high contrasts, the colors are soft pastels with silvery tonalities like tinted photographs, and the landscape is decoratively patterned against the heads of the women. These paintings, more intimate in scale (48″ × 32″) and decorative in composition than the monumental canvases, suggest the personal and feminine aspects of Rosa's personality. They center upon the love Rosa shared with her close women friends.

In *Demonstration*, 1982 (fig. 17), *Procession*, 1983 (fig. 18), and *Voices*, 1983 (fig. 1), Stevens presented not Rosa, but Rosa's legacy—the mass demonstrations that accompanied her death and that still accompany her memory in Germany. In *Demonstration*, Stevens depicted a nearly contemporary event, a demonstration that took place in 1967 in Berlin to commemorate the anniversary of Luxemburg's and Liebknecht's deaths. In Germany, regular demonstrations recall the memory of these two martyrs who have been adopted as symbols of the antinuclear, peace, and socialist movements.

The painting is divided by an erect banner, opposing the images of Liebknecht and Luxemburg carried by the marchers. Rosa's image is brought forward by highlighting against a darker ground, while the image of Liebknecht is slightly obscured by shadow. The son of a prominent German socialist and representative to the General Assembly, Liebknecht served as a highly-respected symbol of German socialism. The legacy of Luxemburg is much more complicated—a Pole by birth,

a Jew, and a woman, she was and remains an interloper in German history. Stevens places the image of Luxemburg in the foreground of contemporary politics.

In *Procession*, the image of Rosa recedes into the background, inscribed with the now famous passage from her last published article in *Die Rote Fahne*, "Ich war, ich bin, ich werde sein" (I was, I am, I will be).[49] Her portrait, presented in high contrast (not unlike those in the collages), reads as a documentary image when compared to the powerful expressionist imagery of the crowd. As the placard with her portrait recedes, the masses who marched at her funeral are crowded close to the picture plane. The harsh contrasts of dark and light within the rich palette of brown and bronze and the painterly expressionist surfaces throb with agitation, movement, and intermittent forces as the marchers are propelled forward by the image of the martyred revolutionary. Obscured by a surface of active brushwork, shadows of her written words can just be glimpsed in the background, providing a visual link to the central motif of *Voices*, in which these same words become powerfully articulated.

When speaking of *Voices*, Stevens states:

> Rosa has gotten smaller in these paintings—and finally disappeared here. Her meaning has become absorbed into the painting, into the context and the resonance of her life. She is her afterimage.[50]

In this image, only the coffins are present, whitened, highlighted against the dark mass of the procession. The figures are compressed into the lower portion of the canvas, anchoring the image with black, white, and subtle greys. Resounding throughout the upper portion of the canvas are Rosa's words: "Ich war, ich bin, ich werde sein." The phrases sing triumphantly in a flickering of blues, magentas, golds, and greens. Seemingly endless layers of words emerge from the silvery background, referring not only to the revolution but also to the memory of Rosa. These paintings of marches and processions, coarsened with molten figures, proclaim through the screen of movement and time the legacy of Rosa Luxemburg. The conspiracy of silence has been broken; history has been re-engaged and lives in the present. These paintings assert

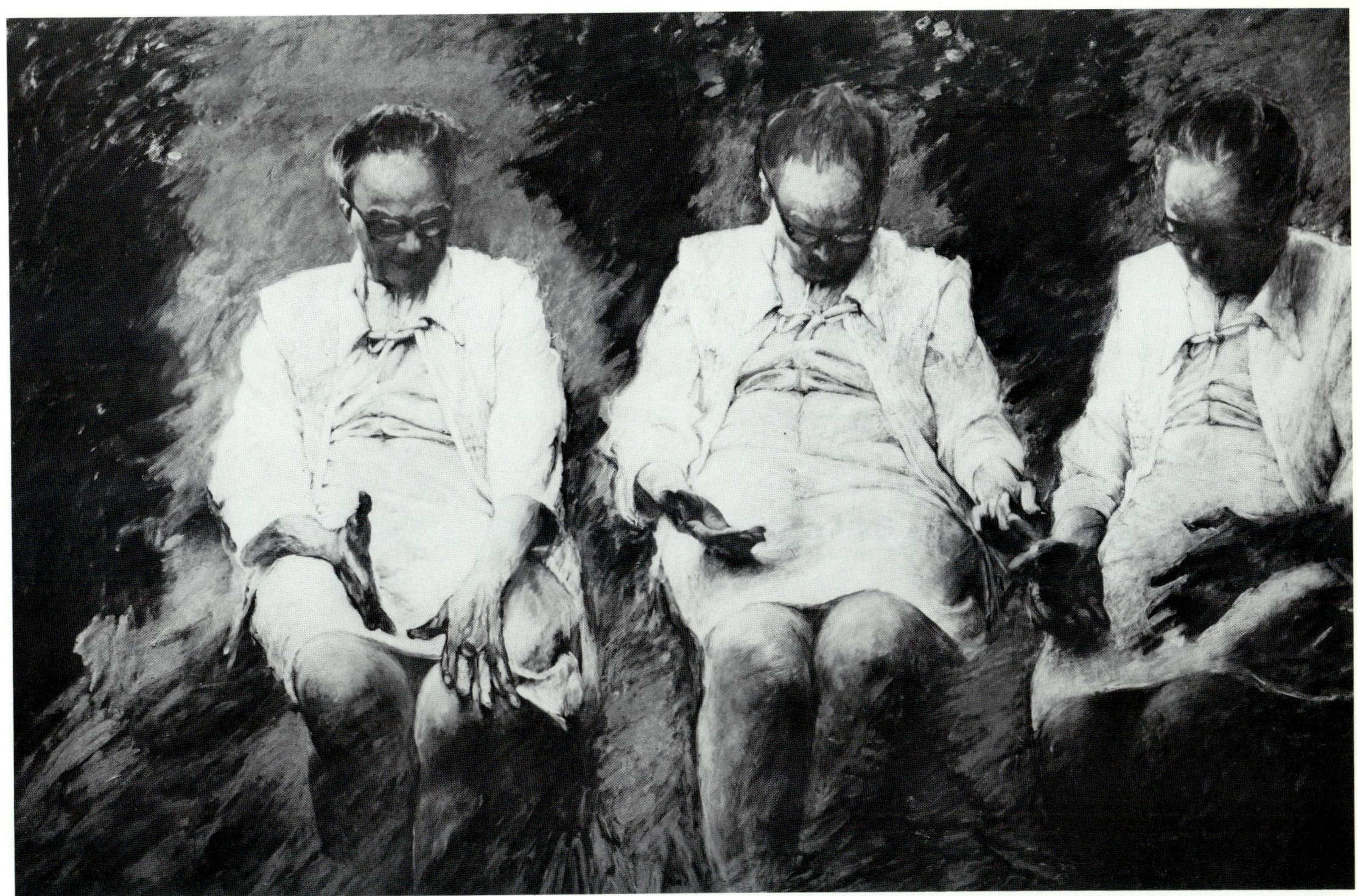

Fig. 14. *Signs*, 1985, acrylic/canvas, 77.5 × 117 ″, Coll. of the artist.

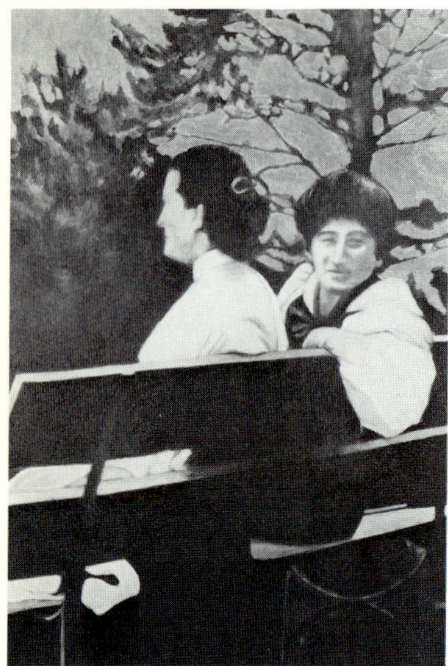
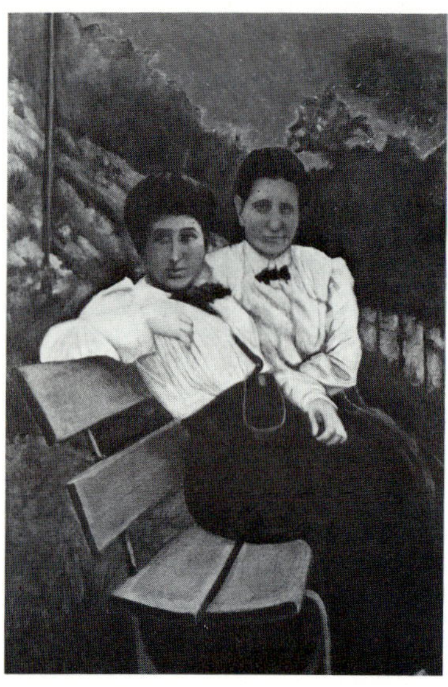

Fig. 15. *Dreams and Theories I*, 1981, acrylic/canvas, 48 × 32″, Coll. of the artist.

Fig. 16. *Dreams and Theories II*, 1981, acrylic/canvas, 48 × 32″, Coll: Elizabeth Hess and Peter Biskind.

Stevens' belief that Rosa's death is not an ending, but an unfinished story.[51]

The voices that dominate these canvases stand in direct opposition to the images of silence comprised in the paintings of Alice.[52] However, in *Forming the Fifth International*, 1985 (fig. 3), Alice and Rosa sit together against the rich green of a landscape setting, actively engaged in dialogue. Alice hugs the picture plane, presented with detailed precision, her physical presence almost tangible. She leans forward, seeming to move freely into the viewer's space. But at the same time, she looks away, unable (or unwilling) to communicate in this world, and turns her attention to Rosa with whom she speaks as a friend. Rosa sits upon a park bench, an image appropriated from previous collages and paintings, and turns toward the viewer. She is painted loosely in silvers and greys, the green of the landscape visible through the thin veils of pigment. Although a figure of enormous presence, she lacks palpability and appears almost spirit-like, as if recalled in memory across distance and time. We are drawn to both women, attracted by Alice's tangible presence and Rosa's intense gaze. Indeed, the viewer has become a part of this imaginary dialogue. "Alice and Rosa talking together as *equals*," Stevens explains,

> represent the value of each human life, the complementarity of intellect and instinct, the symbolic joining of body to mind, form to content. The still-great distance (in color, in time) between them admits no easy solution but holds out, tenuously, promise and necessity. A sad humor, illogic, and vague hope play here with utopian intensity.[53]

Through this mysterious communication with Alice, Stevens brings Rosa to life, and in her most recent paintings, *The Murderers of Rosa Luxemburg*, 1986 (fig. 19), and *Rosa Luxemburg Attends the Second International*, 1987 (fig. 4), she begins to re-imagine Rosa's life for us. In *The Murderers*, she appropriates an image of the Freikorps soldiers celebrating Luxemburg's murder, an image that also appeared in several collages. Two tiers of figures emerge from the blackness. The five men in the foreground, shrouded by shadow, are portrait types—the mustached figure to the center, the actual murderer of Luxemburg. The group of soldiers in the background are anonymous figures, facing the

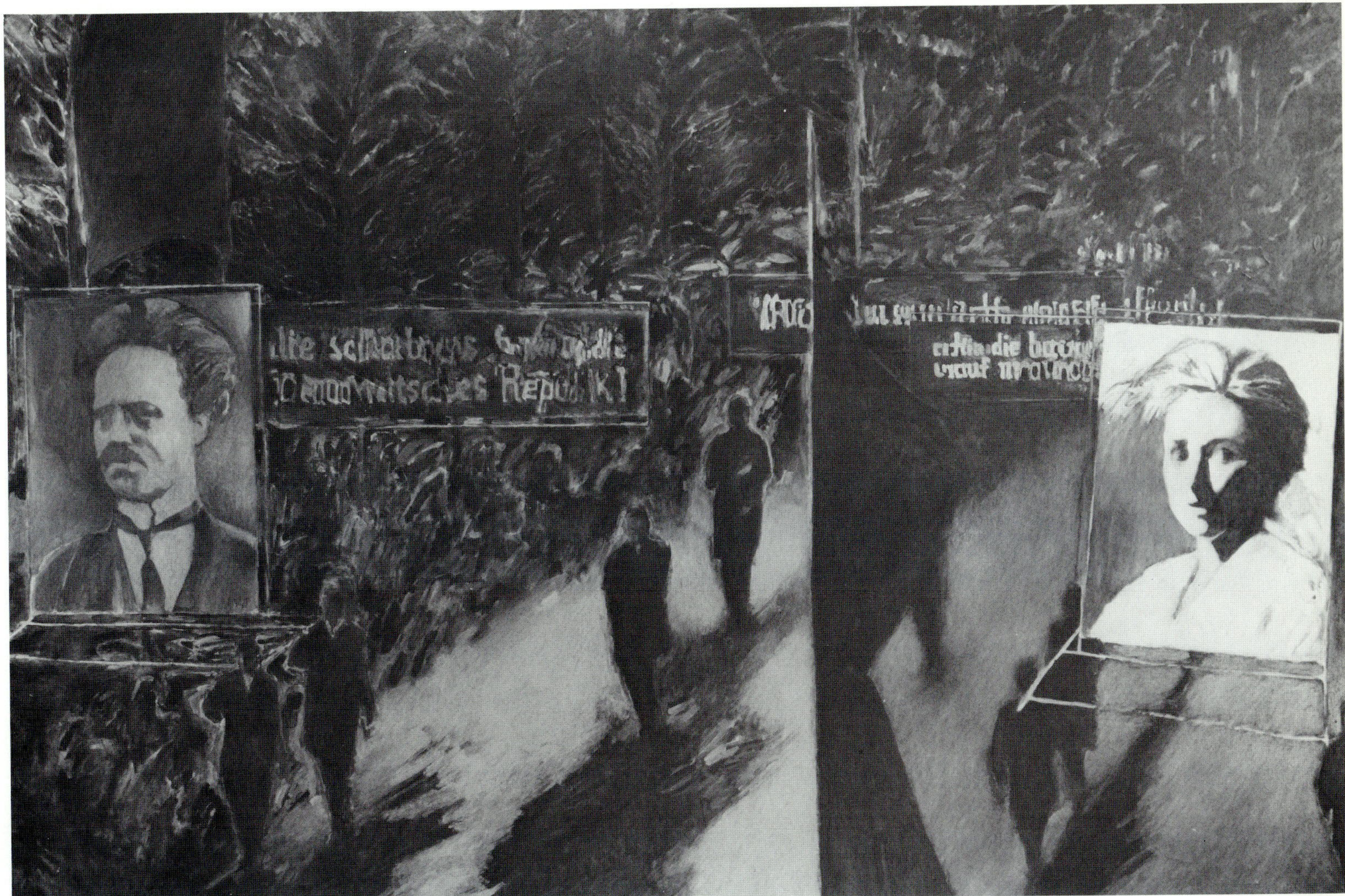


Fig. 17. *Demonstration*, 1982, acrylic/canvas, 78 × 120 ″, private collection.

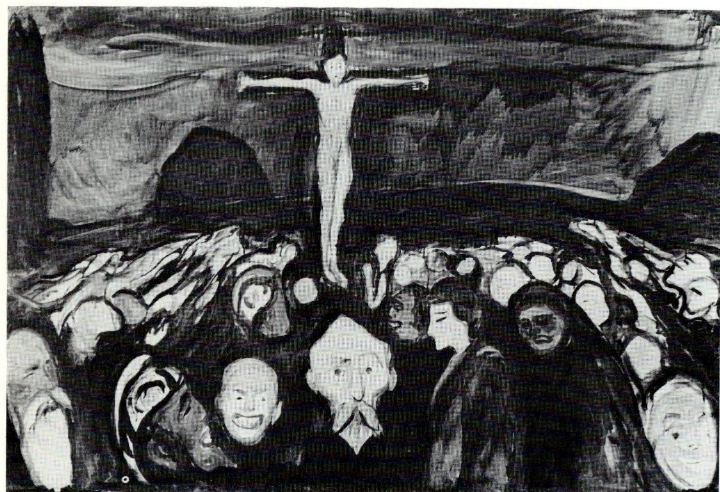

Fig. 20. Edvard Munch, *Golgotha*, 1900, oil/canvas, 32 × 48″, Coll: Munch Museum, Olso.

viewer with skull-like features and deep cavernous eyes. A webbing of red lines runs throughout the background, visually connecting figures while suggesting the vulnerability as well as the culpability of these young men's lives.

Although inspired by a documentary photograph, the painting has a visionary quality, comprised of haunting faces reminiscent of those that inhabit the nightmare worlds of James Ensor, Emil Nolde, and Edvard Munch. In Munch's *Golgotha*, 1900 (fig. 20), for example, spectral faces, distorted and ominous, peer out at the viewer with unrelenting intensity. Similarly, Stevens' threatening painting re-imagines the experience of horror as Luxemburg was knocked to the ground by the rifle butt of her murderer, Otto Runge. Her view of the soldiers louring over her now becomes our view and our experience. The viewer enacts the drama of Rosa's death.

"[These] are paintings of patriarchy . . . It is the woman within patriarchy," Stevens notes.[54] In *The Murderers*, she depicts the villains, the enemies of socialism, while in *The Second International*, she depicts the international socialist guard—the revolutionary leaders. In *The Second International*, the sense of a photographic portrait remains as Stevens retains the rich blacks and greys of the medium. Rosa stands near the center of the painting, engulfed by the sea of male faces that represent the patriarchal order she infiltrated but could never overcome. Nonetheless, she emerges from the crowd by the whiteness of her blouse which bleeds into a discreet area of highlight, by her slightly enlarged scale, and by her central position. With this iconic imagery and hieratic language, Stevens continues to force our attention upon Luxemburg despite the dark and powerful presence of her male colleagues. The domination of the male voice and of men's history are the real subjects here. Experience and effect become one.

The *Ordinary Extraordinary* works synthesize history, politics, sentiment, and experience in a powerful amalgam. As a series, the paintings, collages, and artist's book express the dialectical relationship between Alice and Rosa and the multidimensionality of their characters as re-envisioned by the artist. We, the viewers, bridge the gaps between these disparate realities and make a whole out of the shards of these two

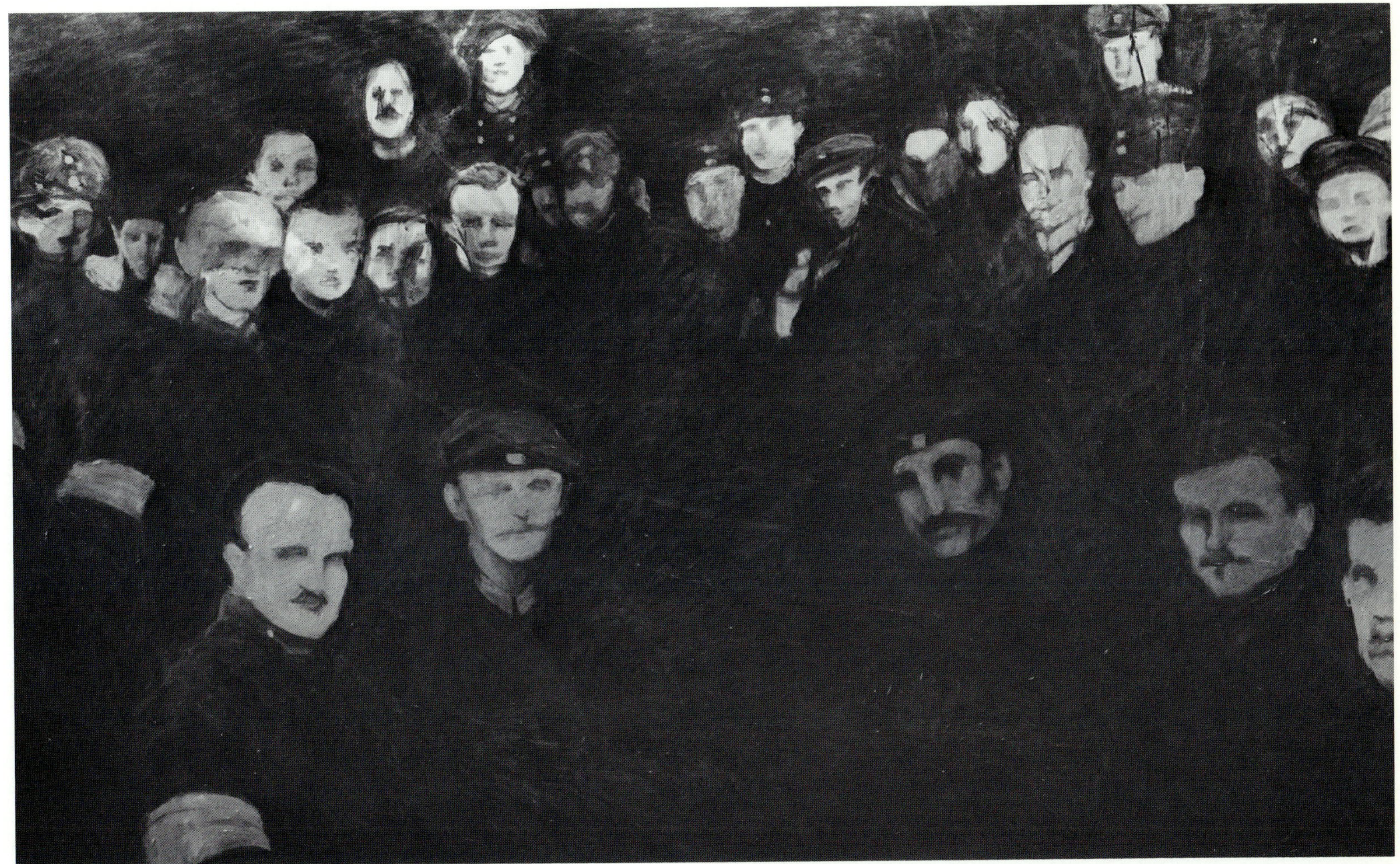

Fig. 19. *The Murderers of Rosa Luxemburg*, 1986, acrylic/canvas, 78 × 129 ", Coll. of the artist.

women's lives. Through this extraordinary series, Alice and Rosa—
and, by extension, all women—have become part of the shared
knowledge of our culture. We understand the political meaning of their
lives. We understand their pain.

May Stevens has been a political artist/activist for thirty-five years. In
addressing those issues of class, race, and gender that most deeply
affected her life, she has taken as her artistic subjects social and political
themes. In her unique poetic style, she recounts her artistic odyssey:
> In my private emotional journey through this swamp, I
> turned to a Jew and a radical and married him
> turned against my Yankee racist father
> publicly painted him as a bigot
> turned toward my Catholic mother
> celebrated her in poems and painted her as companion to
>     Rosa Luxemburg
> turned to Rosa Luxemburg, Jew, radical, as spiritual mother
> bore a half-Jewish son in Europe when the smoke from the ovens
>     was still in the air
> painted the Freedom Riders of the Civil Rights Movement
> painted myself in the place of Courbet/male artist/leader/master
>     surrounded by art world friends and supporters
> painted contemporary women artists as they enter a new role in
>     the history of art.[55]

For Stevens, life, art, and politics are inseparable. In Rosa Luxemburg,
she has found a spiritual mentor, a powerful model, an empathetic
friend. As Rosa lived the revolution, she brought the humanism of her
personal values to the struggle, believing that one truly informed the
other. Similarly, in her art Stevens has long been convinced
> if the ideological input in art is administered in some doctrinaire
> or dutiful way, it doesn't work. This input, that seems to be
> organic, is only valid and powerful when it is first internalized. If
> it is not profound, *deep* in your nature, you're going to get some-
> thing superficial. It has to be *close* to you, very important to
> you . . . When people say words like "political, politics, political
> life," they automatically exclude words like "spiritual, emotional,
> irrational." I think there is great impoverishment in not putting
> them together.[56]

*Ordinary Extraordinary* works on many levels. It is a visual reliquary
of lived experience, capturing the nuances and complexities of human
interaction and consciousness. Yet it presents a powerful political stance,
voicing feminist and socialist concerns to those who wish to hear. The
more we understand the lives of Alice and Rosa, their personal and
political histories, the louder these works proclaim their social message.
For Stevens, these works are like "unopened letters;" they hang in
galleries and museums "testifying that *possibility* lives in art" until their
voices are heard, their political content understood.[57]

# ENDNOTES

[1] Letter to the author dated 6 September 1987.

[2] These paintings and collages were seen for the first time as a major group in the exhibition *May Stevens, Ordinary • Extraordinary, A Summation 1977–1984*, curated by Patricia Hills for the Boston University Art Gallery, 29 February–1 April 1984. The show also traveled to the Art Gallery, University of Maryland, College Park, 24 January–10 March 1985, and the Frederick S. Wight Gallery, University of California at Los Angeles, 7 April–12 May 1985. See the accompanying catalogue for articles by Lucy Lippard, Donald Kuspit, Moira Roth, and Lisa Tickner. The most recent articles to explore the imagery of Alice Stevens are Patricia Mathews, "A Dialogue of Silence: May Stevens' *Ordinary • Extraordinary, 1977–1986*," *Art Criticism* 3, no. 2 (1987): 34-42, and Josephine Withers, "Revisioning our Foremothers: Reflections on the *Ordinary • Extraordinary* Art of May Stevens," *Feminist Studies* 13, no. 3 (Fall 1987): 485-512.

[3] In conversation with the author, MacDowell Colony, Peterborough, New Hampshire, 16 July 1987.

[4] As the historian Edward Hallett Carr wrote, "My first answer therefore to the question, What is history? is that it is a continuous process of interaction between the historian and his facts, an unending dialogue between the present and the past." Carr, *What is History* (New York: Alfred A. Knopf, 1962), 29.

[5] Ann D. Gordon, Mari Jo Buhle, and Nancy Schrom Dye, "The Problem of Women's History," in *Liberating Women's History*, ed. Berenice A. Carroll (Urbana: University of Illinois Press, 1976), 84-85.

[6] Bronner, *Rosa Luxemburg: A Revolutionary for Our Times* (London: Pluto Press, 1981; New York: Columbia University Press, 1987), 7.

[7] Luxemburg's participation in the "revisionism debate" thrust her into the limelight of the international social democratic movement. In her essay "Social Reform or Revolution," she critiqued revisionist theories of Marxism which accepted the contradictions of capitalism and encouraged only modifications of that economic system. Luxemburg, supporting Marx, argued that capitalism was ultimately doomed and sought a new socialist economic structure. For an expanded discussion of this debate see Bronner, 31-41, and J.P. Nettl, *Rosa Luxemburg* (New York: Oxford University Press, 1966), 1:202-251.

The Second International, in existence from 1899 to 1914, was a powerful socialist force in Europe. As an international congress, it believed that certain problems were common to all socialist parties and could be met by common solutions. For the most complete study of this organization, see James Joll, *The Second International 1889–1914* (New York: Harper and Row, 1966).

[8] Bronner, 50.

[9] Bronner, 9.

[10] "The Russian Revolution," 1917, quoted by Bronner, 64-66.

[11] Bronner, 53.

[12] Her spontaneity thesis had three parts: 1) the refusal to subordinate the interests of the class to that of the party; 2) the recognition that socialism could not be realized by decree; and 3) the development of a dialectical relationship between the party and the masses. (Bronner, 40).

[13] Bronner, 86. The book received polemical reviews, both criticized as a misinterpretation of Marx and championed as the most knowledgeable discussion of his theories. (Elzbieta Ettinger, *Rosa Luxemburg: A Life* [Boston: Beacon Press, 1986], 183.)

[14] Quoted by Ettinger, *Rosa Luxemburg*, 183.

[15] Letter to Hans Diefenbach, probably dated 12 May 1917, quoted in Maynard Solomon, *Marxism and Art* (New York: Vintage Books, 1974): 148.

[16] "Order Reigns in Berlin," quoted in Dick Howard, *Selected Political Writings of Rosa Luxemburg* (New York: Monthly Review Press, 1971), 410, 415.

[17] Nettl, 2:773.

[18]The German Communist Party commissioned Mies van der Rohe
(1886–1969), an aesthetically radical but politically unengaged artist, to design
the memorial unveiled on 13 June 1926. Although the party had in mind a clas-
sical monument, van der Rohe suggested a design resembling a brick wall on
the grounds that political victims were often shot against such walls. Moreover,
in its simple arrangement of geometric shapes, it brought to mind a monument of stacked coffins. The inscription, "Ich bin, ich war, ich werde sein,"
was originally superimposed on the facade, but it was removed sometime
before 1931. For more information on this monument, see D.D. Egbert, *Social
Radicalism and the Arts: Western Europe (London: Duckworth Press, 1970), 661-662,
and Franz Schulze, Mies van der Rohe: A Critical Biography* (Chicago: University of
Chicago Press, 1985), 125-128, figs. 79, 80.

[19]An exhibition documenting artists' responses to these two leaders, *Rosa
Luxemburg and Karl Liebknecht • Revolution Remembrance Representation*, was shown
at the Pentonville Gallery in London in 1986. *Voices*, 1983, and *The Murderers of
Rosa Luxemburg*, 1986, by Stevens were included in that exhibition.

[20]Quoted in Raya Dunayevskaya, *Rosa Luxemburg, Women's Liberation, and
Marx's Philosophy of Revolution* (Atlantic Highlands, New Jersey: Humanities
Press, 1981), 95.

[21]Ettinger, *Rosa Luxemburg*, 189.

[22]For more information on Clara Zetkin, see Philip A. Foner, ed., *Clara
Zetkin: Selected Writings*, with a foreword by Angela Y. Davis (New York: International Publishers, 1984).

[23]Howard, 217-218.

[24]Ettinger, *Rosa Luxemburg*, 190.

[25]Quoted in Stevens, *Ordinary. Extraordinary.*, artist's book, n.p., and in part
by Dunayevskaya, 83.

[26]Freud argued that the revolutionary had "unfinished business with his
parental generation" and that he transferred his personal hostility to authority
from the private to the public realm. Moreover, Freud argued that a revolutionary had a "displaced libido," in that he would allow himself no private life
or personal pleasures that would channel his energies away from the revolution. For an extended discussion of this theory see Marie Marmo Mullarmey,
"Gender and Revolution: Rosa Luxemburg and the Female Revolutionary
Personality," *Journal of Psychohistory* 11, no. 4 (1984): 463-476.

[27]*Revolutionary Catechism*, published in 1869. Quoted in Franco Venturi, *Roots
of Revolution* (New York, Grosset and Dunlap, 1966), 365-366, and in Elzbieta
Ettinger, ed. and trans., *Comrade and Lover: Rosa Luxemburg's Letters to Leo Jogiches*

(Cambridge, Massachusetts: The MIT Press, 1979), xv.

[28]Ettinger, *Comrade and Lover*, 73.

[29]Vivian Gornick, "Woman Behind Bars," review of *Rosa Luxemburg: A Life*,
by Elzbieta Ettinger, *The Voice Literary Supplement*, February 1987, 18.

[30]Ettinger, *Comrade and Lover*, xv.

[31]Joan W. Scott, "Gender: A Useful Category of Historical Analysis,"
*American Historical Review* 91 (December 1986): 1054.

[32]Gordon, Buhle, and Dye, 89.

[33]Ettinger, *Rosa Luxemburg*, 119.

[34]Review of *Rosa Luxemburg: A Life*, by Elzbieta Ettinger, *The New York Review
of Books*, 26 March 1987, 3.

[35]In conversation with the author, 16 July 1987.

[36]Wallach, "May Stevens: On the Stage of History," *Arts* 53 (November
1978): 150.

[37]Letter to the author dated 6 September 1987.

[38]In *Mysteries and Politics*, 1978, 78" × 142", Coll: San Francisco Museum of
Modern Art, Stevens first depicted Alice and Rosa in painting. Through this
monumental group portrait, she brought attention to the work of women
activists, such as Betsy Damon, Patricia Hills, and Carol Duncan, while
exploring the compelling mystery of motherhood. In painting, she begins to
bridge the gap between the spiritual and emotional and the political and
intellectual—dichotomies that engage her in the *Ordinary  Extraordinary* works.
For the most comprehensive discussions of this work, see Folke T. Kihlstedt,
"Narrowing the Gap: An Interpretation of Recent Work by May Stevens,"
*Mysteries and Politics: May Stevens*, exh. cat. (Lancaster, Pennsylvania: Dana
Room Gallery, Steinman College Center, Franklin and Marshall College,
1979), and Josephine Withers, "Revisioning our Foremothers." I am grateful
to Josephine Withers for allowing me to read her article in manuscript form.

[39]Several collages serve as variations on this theme, as for example, *Rosa and
Alice*, 1977 (fig. 7), also shown in this exhibition.

[40]Tickner, "May Stevens," in *May Stevens, Ordinary • Extraordinary, A
Summation 1977–1984*, n.p.

[41]Stevens, "My Work and My Working-Class Father," in *Working It Out*,
Sara Ruddick and Pamela Daniels, eds. (New York: Pantheon Books, 1977), 112.

[42]Dunayevskaya, 93.

[43]Stevens, *Ordinary. Extraordinary.*, artist's book, n.p.

[44]See footnote 39.

[45]Indeed, there has been a long-standing relationship between feminism

and the artist's book. The idea of bookart, begun around 1966, was adopted by many women artists who wished to circumvent what they perceived to be a hostile art world. Such artists as Mary Beth Edelson (*Seven Cycles: Public Rituals*), Susan Weil (*Songs/Heartbeats*), and Athena Tacha (*Different Notions of Cleanliness*) are examples of women who used the book as a way to express potent female mythology and intimate autobiographical diaries. For a thorough examination of artists' books, see Deborah Phillips, "Definitely Not Suitable for Framing," *Art News* 80 (December 1981): 62-67.

[46]Letter to the author dated 6 September 1987.

[47]Quoted in Lucy Lippard, "Masses and Meetings," in *May Stevens, Ordinary • Extraordinary, A Summation 1977–1984*, n.p.

[48]Stevens has turned regularly to Gustave Courbet, a nineteenth-century artist, for inspiration during her career. She explained her interest in his painting *Interior of My Studio, a Real Allegory Summing Up Seven Years of My Life as an Artist*, 1854–55, Coll: Musée d'Orsay, Paris:

> In my *Artists Studio [After Courbet, 1974]* I used the tripartite division Courbet used with a group of the artist's contemporaries on either side while he works at the easel. I substituted myself for Courbet, a "Big Daddy" painting for his landscape in progress, my friends for his, and showed the artist seated before *her* easel/canvas. I chose Courbet because I like his paintings and I like his politics, his activism, for which he suffered a great deal. Someday I'd like to work with his *Burial at Ornans* [1849, Coll: Musée d'Orsay, Paris], a great, great painting,

abstractly, ideologically, and in its realistic detail. (Quoted in Lynn F. Miller and Sally S. Swenson, *Lives and Work* [Metuchen, New Jersey: Scarecrow Press, Inc., 1981], 220.) Among those represented in the painting are Sylvia Sleigh, Rudolf Baranik, Nancy Spero, Leon Golub, Lawrence Alloway, and the artist.

[49]When this phrase is singled out from the context of the article "Order Reigns in Berlin," its source in the Book of Revelations 1:8 becomes clear. " 'I am the Alpha and the Omega,' says the Lord God, who is and who was and who is to come, the Almighty." Luxemburg had been reading Revelations shortly before writing this passage.

[50]Quoted from an unpublished transcript of "May Stevens and Donald Kuspit in Dialogue," Boston University Art Gallery, Boston, Massachusetts, 15 March 1984.

[51]In conversation with the author, 16 July 1987.

[52]Mathews, passim. I am grateful to Patricia Mathews for allowing me to read her article in manuscript form.

[53]Letter from Stevens to Josephine Withers dated 9 March 1985, quoted in Mathews, 40.

[54]In conversation with the author, 16 July 1987.

[55]Stevens, "Looking Backward in Order to Look Forward: Memories of a Racist Girlhood," *Heresies* 4, no. 3 (1982): 23.

[56]Quoted in Lippard, n.p.

[57]Stevens, "Taking Art to the Revolution," *Heresies* 3, no. 1, issue 9 (1980): 43.

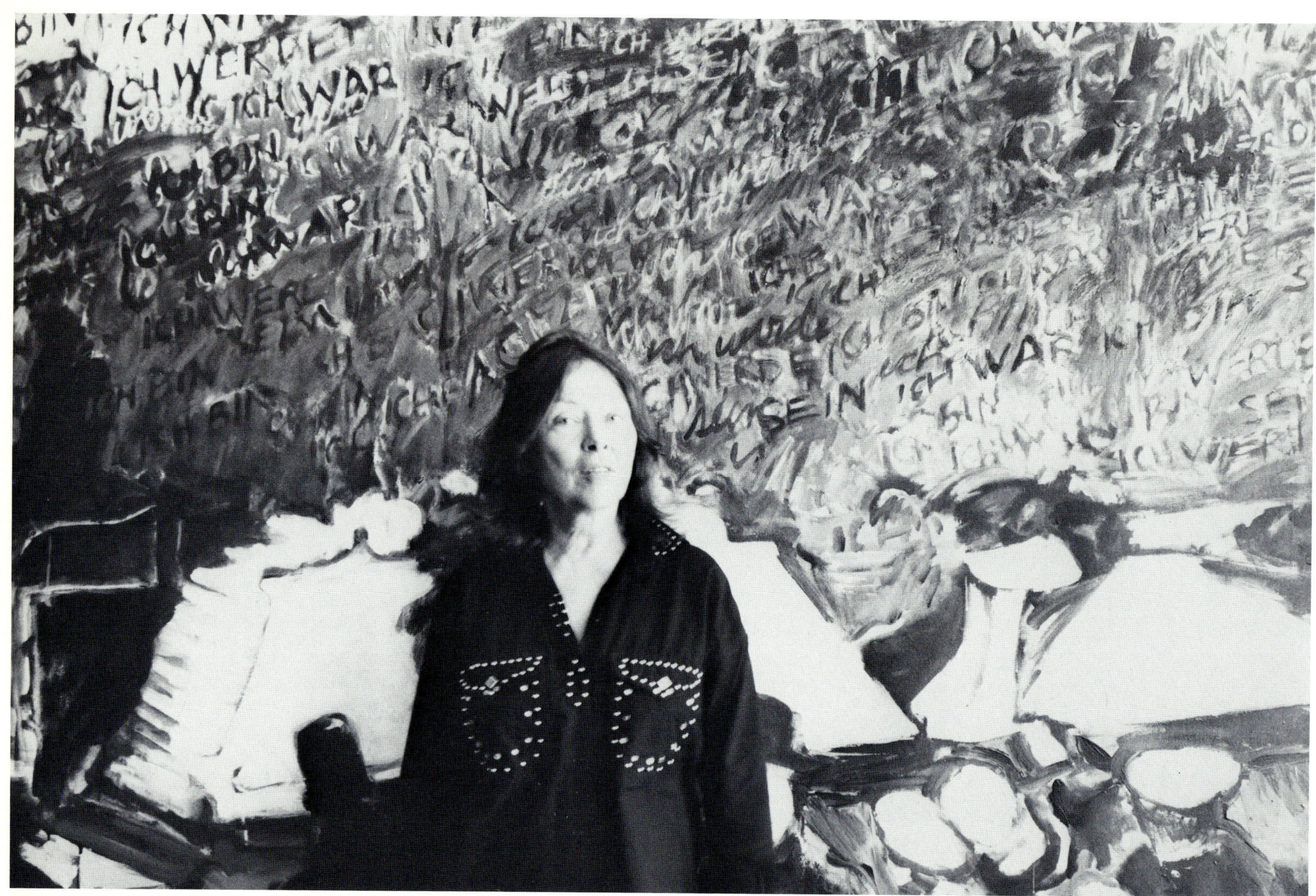

May Stevens stands in front of *Voices*, 1983, in her studio.

JANIS BELL

# *Conversations*

# WITH MAY STEVENS

Along one wall in her Soho studio, May Stevens has hung her small photocollages, xerographs, and some small pieces done by friends. We stood there talking about *Two Women*, 1976 (fig. 5), a collage done for *Heresies* in 1976, and the xerographed image made from it which served as the model for the painting *Everybody Knows Me*, 1981 (fig. 11). I was curious to know why she had started working in xerography and whether she regarded it as a medium with any particular political value.

**Bell:** Why do you work in xerography?

**Stevens:** I like the look of it. I like the degraded photograph very much. I find excitement in the forms that come through. You never know what the machine is going to do. You can treat this medium almost like an abstract expressionist. You just start up and see what happens.

For example, if we compare my graphic work *Ordinary   Extraordinary* with this handmade piece by Harmony Hammond [*Cry*, 1978], the two seem to me to have common qualities, although one is an abstract painting and the other a media reproduction of collaged and painted over photographs. But both have a visual sense, a color sense, a sense of texture and roughness that is similar. I value both of them for those formal reasons, but formal is not separate from other things. One has hand work and one has machine work but I feel the spontaneous,

chance element in both.

**Bell:** Do you take into consideration the fact that it is a less expensive or less exclusive kind of medium when you choose to work in it?

**Stevens:** It's less expensive for me. In terms of its being popular, in having a kind of accessibility—everyone can use a xerox machine—that is part of what gives it its attractiveness. I experience it in terms of the *look*, which I like, but I like that look because of all the atmosphere around it and how many people use it. I sometimes say that going to the xerox machine these days is like going to the well in the old days. Instead of hearing the town gossip at the well, now you meet at the xerox machine, and everybody you know comes in. Also, there's nothing important that you do which you don't duplicate; you never write anything without making a photocopy.

**Bell:** What happens to the "original" if anybody can make a photocopy of your work without "changing" the original?

**Stevens:** The concept of originality is really in question, isn't it?

Most of Stevens works are large oil and acrylic canvases, museum-sized in scale, a traditional genre of art that immediately brings to mind the concept of the "masterpiece" and evokes images of great historical figures such as Courbet, Rembrandt, and Hals. It fits into the "high art" concept, which has been under fire from feminists and political leftists as elitist and patriarchal.[1] I wanted to understand how May Stevens has reacted to this challenge, how she has reconciled her activity in this area with her strong feminist and socialist values. I asked her to elaborate on her statement in *Artforum* (1975) in which she criticized the preoccupation with artistic media.[2]

**Stevens:** I was really writing out of a feeling that I have against those who take John Berger[3] to the ultimate, who say that it is impossible to use oil painting in this day, arguing that because oil painting has been appropriated by the bourgeoisie, oil paintings are about the acquisition of property, and there's no way you can make meaningful art using oil. That's ridiculous. Oil paint is just a medium. A medium is a medium. A medium is not tainted by its owner or its user. It's mystification to say that oil paint is corrupt. I find that such ideas still show up in contemporary thought. Victor Burgin, Mary Kelly, Marie Yates, and Hans Haacke imply that *the* medium to use is photo and text—anything but oil paint—that phototext is the medium for political art and that oil paint is not capable of carrying that message anymore. But I disagree. I think that it is giving medium a primacy it doesn't deserve. I will use paint, photographs, and reproductive equipment like xeroxing in any way that suits me. I feel as though I'm not governed by existing media, that I can pick and choose. They're all there for me.

Stevens sees herself free to explore whatever direction she chooses without concern for what is "in" and, moreover, free to explore more than one direction simultaneously. She talked frequently about the limitations of categories and the falseness and arbitrariness of dichotomies.

**Stevens:** There's this kind of split, this dichotomy. There is mystery and politics, there is Rosa and Alice, there is ordinary/extraordinary, there is mind/body.[4] But that's not really true; that's too simple—because ordinary/extraordinary doesn't mean Rosa/Alice. I've taken that up, but I don't like that split, and I don't approve of it. And so I want to switch places and mix them up, and make them work across each other. There's that wonderful quote from Adrienne Rich,[5] in which she says,

> The rejection of dualism, of the positive-negative polarities between which most of our intellectual training has taken place, has been an undercurrent of feminist thought. And rejecting them, we reaffirm the existence of all those who have through the centuries been negatively defined: not only women, but the "untouchable," the "unmanly," the "nonwhite," the "illiterate," the "invisible" which forces us to confront the problem of the essential dichotomy: power/powerlessness.

I'm trying to put together, to reconcile, and to take what's valuable from each.

I don't want to fuzz everything. But on the other hand, I often have the feeling that the names we give things are attempts to hold onto them, attempts (in a way) to stop a flow of reality, a flow of changing reality, a flow of layered, changing reality. So we give it a name. But almost before the sound of the voice is over, that reality is different than when we started; and furthermore there are so many exceptions, and so many threads that connect that named thing to all different, excluded ways. So what I don't like and what I avoid is holding myself to some sort of definition. I guess I feel that that's not a living thing to do; it's not alive—to take a definition that will exclude things I cannot exclude. I've said things like: "If I have two ideas that are contradictory, and they both seem to be valid, I will not give them up!" I can't.

One of the places I learned this was in the women's movement. In the women's movement we organized, discussed theory, extended all kinds of practice, all without knowing where we were going, and we did this in a sea of contradictions. We couldn't define feminism; some of us defined it one way, some of us defined in other ways. We knew, though, that we did not want to be exclusive. We knew we needed the strength, and the variety, and we needed to fight it out and work it out—not to say, "This is feminism. You go hold your meeting some place else because you don't agree with us!" So we treated it like a living thing. We had a strong *sense* of direction but it was very general. We didn't know for certain how it was going to turn out; we didn't know if there is a feminine aesthetic or not; we tried the idea that maybe there was, and we had to discard it. But we tested it.

It seems that this is the way I work in my painting, and this is the way I work in my thinking and in my life. I have these ideas and I try them and I test them, and I use them as long as they are working. When they don't work anymore I rethink them. Sometimes if the idea doesn't work, I make it expand. Or eventually maybe I give up on it.

I believe you have to live in flux. You have to live without solid, secure, continuous bases. Because that's not the way the world is.

**Bell:** Is that why you emphasize ambiguity in your work, even on a formal level? Is that why in *Heresies*,[6] you identified the value of art with its property of being "amorphous and infinitely variable?"

**Stevens:** I don't think it's all knowable; and what I do know may be different tomorrow. And I have to live with that. But I have enough sense of certainty and self to be comfortable with that.

Since about 1977, Stevens' work has been primarily a series called *Ordinary Extraordinary*, exploring images of her mother, Alice Stevens, and the Polish/German revolutionary Rosa Luxemburg. Most of the large canvases have treated either Rosa or Alice separately from one another; however, some of the collages and xerographs in her artist's book juxtaposed images of both, and a recent painting, *Forming the Fifth International*, 1985 (fig. 3), brought Rosa and Alice into the same pictorial space. Since Melissa Dabakis in her essay traces the development of Stevens' ideas on Rosa and, consequently, the evolution of the style in which Stevens has stated these ideas, I asked Stevens to explain why she works in series and how she expects individual images to be perceived with regard to the larger body of work in each series.

**Bell:** What is the importance to you of working in a series.
**Stevens:** I was just thinking it's consistent with things I've said earlier about bringing together apparent opposites. I don't do series as a programmatic thing. I have never decided that I'm going to do a series on a particular theme. Usually I start with an idea that's interesting to me and, almost always, I do several of them. I get charged up and it never works for me to do one. For example, when I was asked to do some work for the *Attica Book*,[7] I did three pieces and they only needed one. One was published, and then I had two others that I used as regular art pieces. So it always happens that I have several pieces whenever I do anything. Similarly with the major series.

It just happens that there is always another idea, another aspect, another way of handling it. I guess what really happens is that there are alternatives and I would like to try them. I always feel that I can only predict and foresee to a certain extent, and then I have to do it. It's almost like writing a poem in your head that works up to a certain point, but then you have to write it down to bring it to completion. It's the same thing with a work of art: I have to make it physical to see it and know what it is. And then, in making choices, I decide, "Well, I'll go in this direction with this one; but then there is the optional idea, so I'll do that next." *Big Daddy* and then *Ordinary Extraordinary* developed out of a need to say more, and to say differently, and to pursue further an idea.

**Bell:** What about the experience of a viewer seeing a work out of the context of its series, for example, on the wall of a museum?
**Stevens:** My work is conceived as it goes and ends up being a series. It's not meant to be a series like parts of a continuing sentence. They're meant to be, and I think they are, "looks" at a situation from slightly different angles. The process is analogous to molding a sculpture in the round, going around it, each time giving it a nudge and shaping it. So with the tractable material that I want to get into, understand, and make known, I try to approach it from different angles. Each work is a "looking at it" from a different angle. Now it's possible that several works may end up looking at it from the same angle. I think they add to each other a great deal, but I think they can also be seen as individual works.

The other thing that is relevant is that I often think about film. I see these ideally in an installation as making a progression, moving through

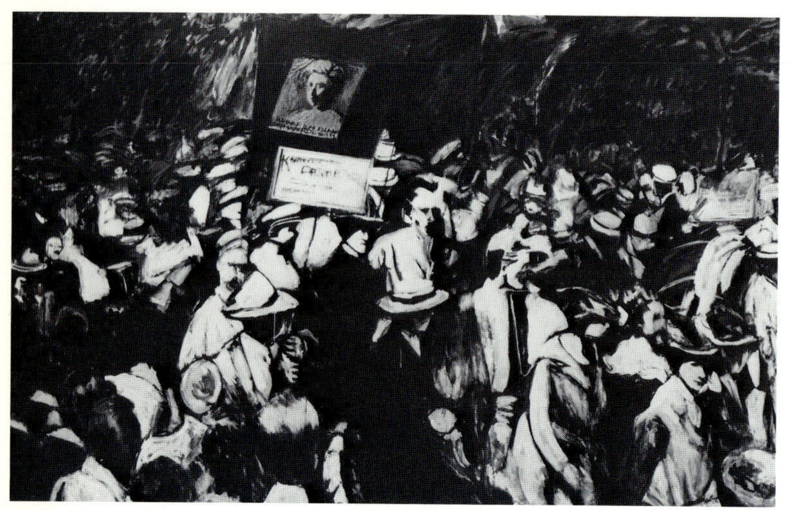

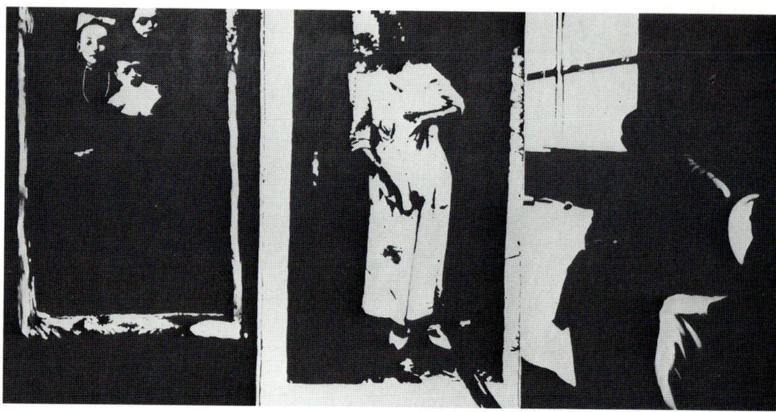

time and space and experience. I'm fully aware of their very cinematic sense. Also, even in paintings that have the same figure three times, there is that cinematic quality—of stopped time. I spent my childhood at the movies; when I wasn't reading I was at the movies. Actually the size of my paintings has a lot to do with the desire for the movie screen. When I sit in front of a movie screen and I'm waiting for the picture to go on, I look at the shape of that screen and I think, "My God, wouldn't my painting look good up there!"

Now the problem to which I was referring when I wrote that art becomes more formal on a museum wall is different.[8] When art is created in its time and in its context, it has a kind of vitality that comes from the energy that made it happen, the fact that it's going to mix with things in the society and stir things up. It is part of a living history, and especially if it's political work, it might stir things up. But even that work which might be very political, when hung on the wall of a museum in isolation is going to become part of that wall, fade onto that wall and stay there, and become a more formal piece. The issue that gave rise to

that work will fade; maybe it won't be resolved, but it will no longer be a pointed issue. Still the work will have other meanings if it is a complex work of art. So that's why I say that the work will change its meaning, and the formal elements will perhaps be more salient when the precise issue is no longer on the agenda.

Stevens' concern with formal problems was evident as she showed me her works and talked about her working methods. She finds excitement in discovering and refining her ideas during the process of working, a concept of process that derives from her early exposure to abstract expressionism. In a letter of 31 August 1987, she defined the working process in abstract expressionism in the same spirit as she spoke of her own creative process:

> I see abstract expressionism as . . . basically concerned with the creation of new and unexpected relationships. Accidents are made or found or allowed to happen (i.e., set up). They are then brought

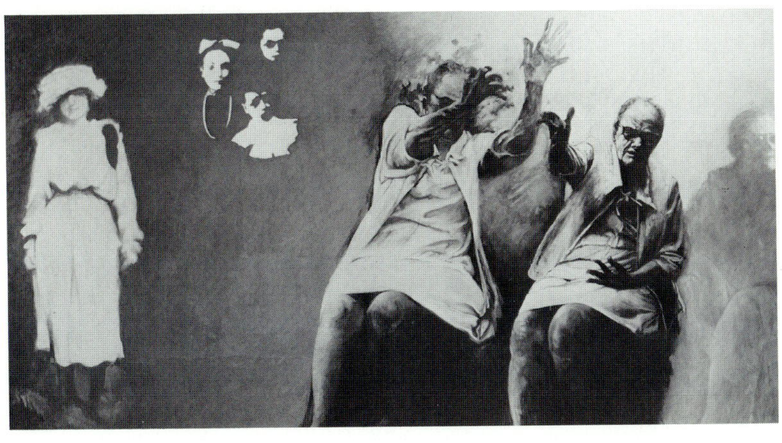

Fig 18. *Procession*, 1983, acrylic/canvas, 78 × 120″, Coll. of the artist.

Fig. 11. *Everybody Knows Me*, 1981, acrylic/canvas, 78 × 142″, Coll: Fraunces B. and Eugene Gorman.

Fig. 13. *Go Gentle*, 1983, acrylic/canvas, 78 × 142″, Coll. of the artist.

into relationships with all other events occurring in the picture space by the creation of more accidents and/or the elimination of others. It is a curious mixture of letting go, giving over to chance, and retaining a latent control.

Stevens rarely works from preliminary sketches, although she showed me three oil sketches from which *Fore River* (fig. 12) evolved. Originally focusing on a bridge over the canal in which Luxemburg's body was found, Stevens worked up the silvery/pewter tones of the central area until the bridge was only a phantom, a luminous void connecting the two images of Alice. She described the process of discovery as one of watching the bridge fade out and the painting come to life. Analyzing the formal function of the grey vertical as it shifts from solid to void, alternately advancing and receding, Stevens remarked that "even now, the presence of the fall of silver in the center seems to me more mysterious and compelling than I can say."

Stevens is intrigued by the glittery quality of silver and other metallic colors and has explored ways to integrate them with matte colors in her work. Laughingly pointing to a pair of silver canvas shoes on her feet, she explained how she thinks glitter has been inappropriately categorized in our culture as "superficial"; rather, it is something out there, beckoning to be used. She explained that she wanted to use it for the ground of *A Life*, 1984 (fig. 2), but had to discard this idea when it wouldn't work with the color and forms of the figures.

**Stevens:** *A Life* originally had iridescent silver and pewter tones for the ground, which was wrong, because the figures of Alice couldn't merge into it; it was too bright. So now the ground is a rare mixture of umbers, purples, and blues; I layered, worked over it, and adjusted it to a little bit more brown, or a bit more blue, or violet, to make it vibrate. The rest of the painting, on the other hand, came right away and is barely overpainted.

Both *A Life* and *Signs*, 1985 (fig. 14), are "triptychs," creating a cinematic and discursive quality through repetition, framing, and scale. I asked Stevens to talk about these formal concerns.

**Stevens:** Scale is important in my work; I deliberately choose lifesize and over-lifesize figures. I work with the canvases on the wall at a height of about eight inches off the floor. The figures are at eye level; you enter their space, and they seem to come out and confront you.

I've often thought about the question of why three figures and not one. If a single gesture is kind of a word or communication, then the whole painting is a sentence.

**Bell:** It's clear that the traditional dichotomy in art history between form and content—or style and iconography—is a totally inappropriate way of talking and thinking about your work. How do you work out the problems of going from ideation to realization, of finding the visual forms for your ideas, to the extent that those ideas can even be thought of separately from their visual form?

**Stevens:** I obviously don't see form as contradictory to content. It seems to me that a very full, deep, rich, heavy content simply requires equivalent formal means. I want them to balance each other. I don't want the content to take over. I think the danger is that the content will take over. I think about the formal all the time, not for its own sake, but rather to get where I want to get to. It's very exciting to fight it out and to make it work with the content, because it's that adventurous part again where it's not foreknown, but where you know when it's right. When it works, everything clicks. When the formal falls into place, the content reaches its fullest power.

**Bell:** You've been talking about resonances of meaning and the bringing together of opposites; these concepts seem evident in your work in formal terms as well.

**Stevens:** One word I use in talking about my work is that it's sort of chunky. It has solid pieces in it, and they don't always get totally absorbed in the thing. So there is disjunction. And in a way it's absolutely necessary and important that some disjunction remain. If I'm putting together disparate things, I don't want them to be non-disparate. I don't want them to be resolved in total harmony.

**Bell:** Can you elaborate on that in some particular works?

**Stevens:** In *A Life*, the figure of Alice is squeezed into the canvas in an uncomfortable way; her elbows and knees are cramped; there's not much space for her to be comfortable in; she's kind of wedged, and at one point the elbows of two figures actually overlap and they seem to nudge each other. There's very delicate fine work in some of the features, veins of the hands, and folds of the dress, but there is also a kind of broadness in the drawing and in the basic shapes of the body. I think that I often move from delicacy to brusqueness, and many of my shapes are heavy and not graceful. But on the other hand, there is a lot of balance and flow in spite of the fact that the shapes may be kind of klutzy and clumpy.

In *Voices*, 1983 (fig. 1), the upper area is quite loose, merging and emerging, but the bottom area is highly structured and geometrical. I think there is a lot of disjunction in having small articulation of the letters and no clear structure, and on the bottom having—almost like a woodcut—fiercely separated segmentation.

How Stevens regards this disjunction as a vehicle for meaning is further clarified by juxtaposing these ideas with previous statements delivered at the Boston University Art Gallery in 1984.[9] Here she explained how meaning is conveyed by form and color in *Voices* and then in *Fore River:*

> *Voices*: The sight of two coffins carried through the street, a sight so simple, so awful, is like the primal scene, the beginning of something we do not understand. Black and white figures surround the coffin shapes, the coffins more animate than individual men and women who become the crowd, turned away and to the side . . . Overhead Rosa's last words . . . pile up, turn and fall and rise. They are like sounds. They make a vaulted space or a series of vaultings for the sound to resonate in . . .

*Fore River*: Alice sits on either side of the river . . . She examines her hands or speaks with them, making signs. The movement of her hands is like the flicker of overlapping letters, characters in *Voices*—small articulations spelling out impulses to be read or heard. These gestures cross the central void and tie into the larger, vaguer hand in the root growths, the artist's hand.

When one glances back and forth from *Voices* to *A Life* and *Signs*, the obvious differences in color, composition, gesture, and surface treatment cannot be interpreted according to the traditional art historical notion of a "stylistic development" from 1983 to 1985. The character of Stevens' works from 1985 to 1987, such as *The Murderers of Rosa Luxemburg*, 1986 (fig. 19), and *Rosa Luxemburg Attends the Second International*, 1987 (fig. 4), confirmed this. I was interested in the fact that Rosa had lurked in the background of the earlier works (to 1983) as a spiritual presence—an unreachable, insubstantial ideal. Although she had begun to take on a physical presence in *Forming the Fifth International*, she still lacked the naturalism of chromatic color.

**Bell:** Would you talk about the differences between the "Rosa" and the "Alice" paintings? It's clear that you're finding a different visual form for different statements, all of which reminds me of the seventeenth-century artist/writer Bellori's concept of the "idea"—that the content has to correspond to the visual form, that whatever is done with form affects meaning.

**Stevens:** That issue is absolutely central and an idea not confined to a single historical period. It's like the difference between summarizing what one wants to say and saying what one wants to say. And I'm horrified that I sometimes find myself summarizing what a particular painting is about! It's like naming and boxing, categorizing, not understanding that the form is *not superfluous*. The feeling that people often seem to have is that a concern with form means that you don't really care about what you're saying, you don't care about people, you don't care about humanity. But *form* is the medium. The medium is form, not paint, or drawing, or graphic work.

**Bell:** The "Alice" paintings certainly use more color than the "Rosa" paintings; their use of design and other formal qualities is different, and I think the attention of critics suggests that people have found them more gripping.

**Stevens:** I think perhaps the most powerful "Alice" picture doesn't use much more color than the "Rosa" pictures (I'm referring to *Go Gentle*, 1983 [fig. 13]). One thing that may be interesting to think about is the separate development of the two tracks, so to speak, about what has happened to the images as they have been worked on. I think that Alice has gotten closer and more real than she was originally. And what I've been saying about Rosa is that it seems to me that she has continued to be in her historical environment; she's sort of dispersed. Maybe in this one [*Forming the Fifth International*] I'm trying to make her come more to the fore, but she still doesn't—quite.

**Bell:** But she does seem to be coming more to life in the sense that you started with her already dead, and you're working your way back into her life.

**Stevens:** Right, but in some sense this painting [*Forming the Fifth International*] is much more alive than that one [*Rosa Luxemburg Attends the Second International*].

**Bell:** The surface is more alive, but the image of Rosa isn't; she really makes contact with the viewer in *Rosa Luxemburg Attends the Second International*. I think we empathize more with Rosa in the latter.

**Stevens:** There is another formal issue here, though. I can't do certain things with Rosa. There are things I'd like to do to Rosa, ways I'd like to use her in paintings, that I can't do. And I can't do them because it doesn't feel as if I know her well enough, or I understand her; I can't play games with her, I can only treat her with a certain kind of respect and understand her as much as I understand her. I can't falsify or force it. If I were taking this whole project less seriously, then I could put Rosa wherever, I could do anything with her. But to put her here with Alice [*Forming the Fifth International*], which is the most radical thing I've done with her, is very difficult. And I think they're there in a very uneasy fashion. It's because that's the truth of it—that their relationship is awkward and uneasy, one that doesn't quite make it. But at least

they're trying! They're there together in this green environment.
I look at it and I think, "Rosa is an idea." But the eccentricity and the
poignancy is all there. That's why—how—it works.

**Bell:** You talked yesterday about wanting to do more with Rosa,
wanting to "deconstruct her" and make her come more alive. Is that the
direction you see now?

**Stevens:** I would like to. The question is, what can Rosa be for me,
me as a tester, as someone who is paying close attention? She could, as
she does, exist in other manifestations of her sensibility and vision. She
can only be in whatever resonances there are of her having lived, and
the ways in which those resonances are still active. But I don't know
what that means. That's the project or the problem: is there a way of
making Rosa live through what there is now that she can be seen as
having made happen? That's my formulation, but I have to discover
what it means visually.

It's fun to invent possibilities for myself. I've often thought up paintings I didn't do. What novelists often say is that they create a set of
characters and watch how they interact. In a way it's like that for me.
Sometimes I get tired of doing the same thing, I'd like to do something
else, but it would have to grow naturally. I would have to grow into it.

New York City, September 1987

# ENDNOTES

[1] See Thalia Gouma-Peterson and Patricia Mathews, "The Feminist
Critique of Art History," *Art Bulletin* 69 (September 1987): 326-357, for an
overview of the literature on this issue.

[2] Stevens, *Artforum* (September 1975): 35-36: ". . . Primacy of medium is a
false issue, a diversion. It's easier to deal with the problems of media and
subject matter than with those of art."

[3] Berger, *Ways of Seeing*, BBC and Penguin Books, 1977.

[4] *Mystery and Politics* is also the name of a painting by Stevens (Coll. San
Francisco Museum of Art). The dichotomies "Rosa Alice" and "Ordinary
Extraordinary" refer also to series and exhibitions by Stevens.

[5] Rich, *Of Women Born* (New York: Bantam Books, 1976), p. 48.

[6] Stevens, "Taking Art to the Revolution," *Heresies* 3, no. 1 (1980): 40-43.

[7] Benny Andrews and Rudolf Baranik, eds., *Attica Book* (New York: The
Black Emergency Cultural Coalition and The Artists and Writers Protest,
1973). Stevens writes: "The book consists of art by forty-eight artists, equally
divided between black and white, all addressing the prison rebellion in a maxi-
mum security installation in upstate New York. It also included poetry by
prisoners. One of the pieces made by Stevens was based on the image of
George Jackson and a fragment of a letter Jackson wrote from prison to
Angela Davis. This piece was shown in 1984 at the Studio Museum in Harlem
in the 'Traditional and Conflict' exhibition, which traced the responses of
black artists to their political history. A few white artists were also included."

[8] Stevens, *Heresies*: 43.

[9] Unpublished transcript of "May Stevens and Donald Kuspit in Dialogue,"
Boston University Art Gallery, Boston, Massachusetts, 15 March 1984.

# A THIRD PRESENCE

In November 1982, a close friend of mine died unexpectedly; she was murdered. The shock of losing this friend penetrated the deepest layers of my being, unloosening long-repressed pain surrounding the death of my father (some twenty years earlier), and all of a sudden, I was grieving the loss of two people. The winter months that followed were a time of solitude, pain and uncontrollable emotions. When the spring arrived I was a different person. The sadness remained, but it had evolved. An excerpt from my journal of that period describes some of the feeling:

> . . . And I'm falling again in another wave of sadness. But this time it is a sorrow without suffering, a sorrow mysteriously bright, one so healing that I feel a change within each of my cells.

During the winter I was working on a book. Two or three evenings of each week I cleared enough space in my life to sit down and write. An involuntary ritual developed and continued for almost three months. As soon as I would get my papers together and sit down in my place to work, sadness would begin to well up inside me. The book had nothing to do with the death of my friend or my father, but somehow the act of focusing on my writing triggered the whirling of my sadness. It would build for a couple of minutes and then I would cry. Soon the crying changed into anger. For just an instant, at the peak of the anger, I was out of control, volatile. After this release, the anger subsided and I felt a burst of creative energy and a clear resolve to do my writing.

This emotional pattern occurred so many times that I began to expect and perhaps even cultivate it. The burst of energy that came after the anger was eerie; it felt as though it did not come from me, that it was just passing through me. There was also a twinge of guilt: rationally or not, I somehow traced the source of my bursts of energy to the death of my friend.

Much later, I began to recognize my experience as a small example of an elemental or archetypal pattern. Nothing pressures the human psyche more intensely than death. When an individual (or a community) allows the grief-horror-fear-anger to stream through his or her being, a change takes place on every level—spiritual, mental, emotional, cellular—and a powerful regenerative force is released in response to the death. Oftentimes people report feeling "more alive" in the wake of such experiences. It is a singular energy, different from other creative impulses, and I have learned to recognize it in the mythology and art of every culture.

An artist does not have the freedom to choose this archetype. If anything, it chooses you. The artist's freedom lies in her reaction to death, her willingness or unwillingness to open to the streaming process. Images, once created and placed in the physical world, are autonomous entities with their own power. On subtle levels, images made in response to death can evoke more death (an easy example—the *Rambo* movies in the wake of the Vietnam War) or they can generate new life. In the latter response there is the possibility of a transcendent work, one which

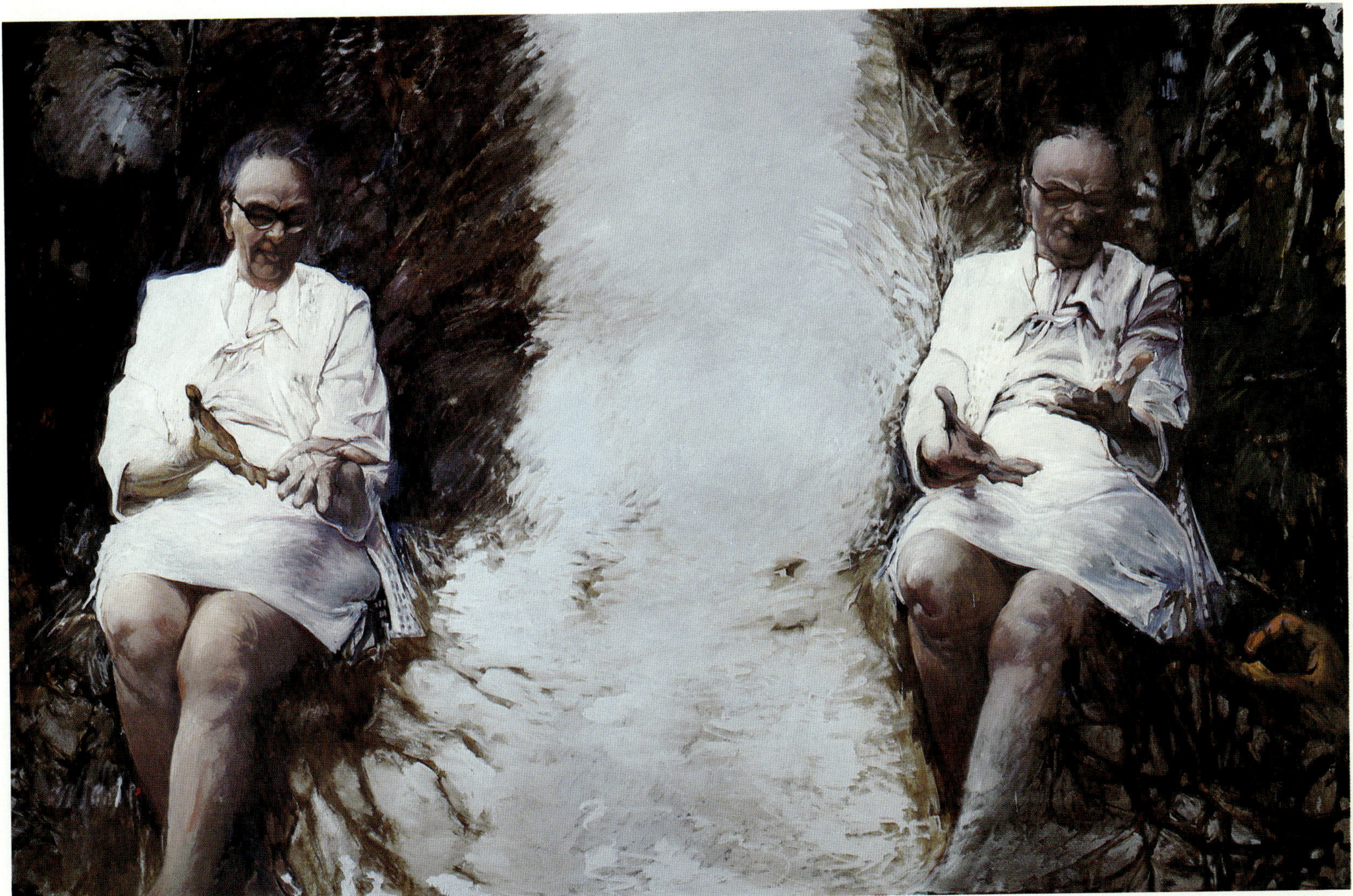

Fig. 12. *Fore River*, 1983, oil/canvas, 78 × 120 ″, Coll. of the artist.

carries wisdom from one generation to the next. In her painting *Fore River*, 1983 (fig. 12), May Stevens has been given the torch to carry. Her series of interrelated paintings titled *Ordinary  Extraordinary*, spanning more than seven years, offers a rare opportunity to see the process of an artist "laboring for the gift."[1]

The form of May Stevens' series, the juxtaposition of her mother, Alice, with Rosa Luxemburg, has been the subject of several valuable essays. However, the discussion of May Stevens' work has come primarily from the "political" mind, and consequently her work has been categorized as "political art," which is accurate, of course, but also far too limiting. This label (in U.S. culture at least) holds the paintings away from a larger audience that might respond to the work primarily on emotional and spiritual levels. Within the political form that she has created, the artist is receiving and giving forth mystical resonances. Her subject is what Mircea Eliade calls "the eternal return,"[2] her teacher is Rosa Luxemburg.

In preparation for this essay, I asked the artist to give me a short selection of Luxemburg's writings. I already had an overview of Luxemburg's life, but I wanted more, and I also knew that the artist's choice of what to give me would be the trailhead to explore deeper into the *Ordinary  Extraordinary* series.

Like Martin Luther King Jr., Gandhi, Tolstoy, and other important historical figures, Luxemburg communicated spiritual wisdom along with political knowledge, as demonstrated by two quotes from the material the artist gave me:[3]

> . . . How strange it is that I am always in a sort of joyful intoxica-
> tion, though without sufficient cause. Here I am lying in a dark
> cell upon a mattress hard as stone; the building has its usual
> churchyard quiet, so that one might as well be already entombed;
> through the window there falls across the bed a glint of light from
> the lamp which burns all night in front of the prison. At intervals I
> can hear faintly in the distance the noise of a passing train or close
> at hand the dry cough of the prison guard as in his heavy boots, he
> takes a few slow strides to stretch his limbs. The grind of the gravel
> beneath his feet has so hopeless a sound that all the weariness and
> futility of existence seems to be radiated thereby into the damp
> and gloomy night. I lie here alone and in silence, enveloped in the
> manifold black wrappings of darkness, tedium, unfreedom, and
> winter—and yet my heart beats with an immeasurable and
> incomprehensible joy, just as if I were moving in the brilliant sun-
> shine across a flowery meadow. And in the darkness I smile at life,
> as if I were the possessor of charm which would enable me to
> transform all that is evil and tragic into serenity and happiness.
> But when I search my mind for the cause of this joy, I find there is
> no cause, and only laugh at myself. I believe that the key to the
> riddle is simply life itself, this deep darkness of night is soft and
> beautiful as velvet, if one only looks at it in the right way. The
> grind of the damp gravel beneath the slow and heavy tread of the
> prison guard is likewise a lovely little song of life—for one who has
> ears to hear. At such moments I think of you, and would that I
> could hand over this magic key to you also. Then at times and in
> all places, you would be able to see the beauty, and the joy of life;
> then you also could live in the sweet intoxication, and make your
> way across the flowery meadow. Do not think that I am offering
> you imaginary joys, or that I am preaching asceticism. I want you
> to taste all the real pleasures of the senses. My one desire it to give
> you in addition my inexhaustible sense of inward bliss.

> Thus passing out of my cell in all directions are fine threads
> connecting me with thousands of creatures great and small,
> whose doings react upon me to arouse disquiet, pain, and self-
> reproach. You yourself, too, belong to this company of birds and
> beasts to which my nature throbs responsive. I feel how you are
> suffering because the years are passing beyond recall without your
> being able really to "live!" Have patience, and take courage! We
> shall live nonetheless, shall live through great experiences. What
> we are now witnessing is the submergence of the old world, day by
> day another fragment sinks beneath the waters, day by day there
> is some fresh catastrophe. The strangest thing is that most people
> see nothing of it, but continue to imagine that the ground is firm

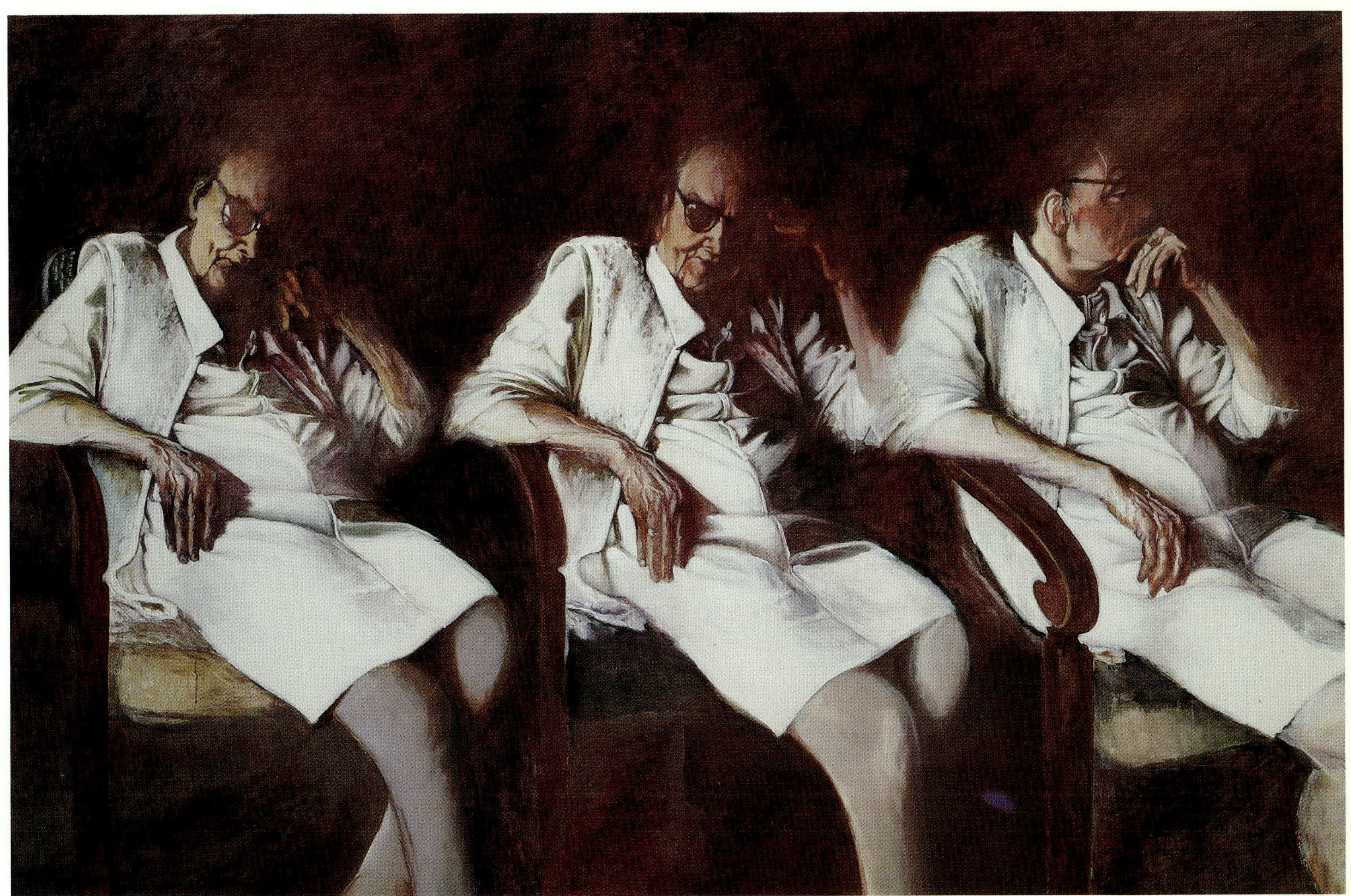

Fig. 2. *A Life*, 1984, acrylic/canvas, 78 × 120″, Coll. of the artist.

beneath their feet.

Luxemburg's leaps of spiritual growth took place in the physical space of a prison cell. May Stevens' leaps took place in the emotional space of grief. In 1981, at the beginning of *Ordinary Extraordinary*, the artist's son, Steven Baranik, died tragically. Unseen, and unknowable to the viewer, Steven Baranik is a third presence in the *Ordinary Extraordinary* series. The artist's connection with his presence and her process of integrating the pain of his physical death catalyze the regenerative energy in the paintings.

The series is most rewarding when one can reflect upon the chronology of the seventeen or so paintings. For the context of this essay, we pick up the narrative in June 1983 and follow it through four paintings to the end of the summer. The artist remembers that time period: "Everyone was away that summer, I had lots of time and I pushed myself very hard." *Go Gentle*, 1983 (fig. 13), started earlier in the year, was put aside half-finished to begin work on *Voices*, 1983 (fig. 1). This painting, which was completed without interruption, is different from any of her previous paintings. The brush strokes are looser, more charged; the images formed more from the body, less from the intellect. Something has shifted in the psyche of the artist. Two years have passed since the death of her son, and in this painting her grief opens to release the regenerative energy. One feels it most directly in the background field above the coffin. The phrase "Ich war, Ich bin, Ich werde sein"[4] is painted again and again in a dark shimmering trance. It is here that the artist established connection with the part of Rosa that is alive, with the part of her son that is alive. The mood is defiant, even victorious; in English the words are "I was, I am, I will be." However this defiance does not take the form of bold images (as in the *Big Daddy* series); rather it is fluid and pervasive. Like water, it is relentless, flowing around any obstacle in its path.

Procession, 1983 (fig. 18), follows immediately after *Voices*. I imagine the artist intoxicated with the discovery of her new energy and wanting more, wanting to immerse herself deeper into the feeling of the rushing river. In *Procession*, the energy of the background field of *Voices* is extended to the entire canvas. The brush strokes loosen up another few notches, she pushes the energy to a crescendo, and the figures in the crowd barely hold their physical shapes.

At this point in the chronology, the artist pulls back into the formal issues of the series and returns to *Go Gentle*, taking with her what was learned energetically in *Voices* and *Procession*. The painting is resolved into a serial portrait of Alice, and stylistically, it is the tour de force of the series, with the artist demonstrating mastery of her two image modalities. What is important in the context of this essay is how the regenerative energy contacted in the two previous paintings changes as the artist shifts her attention from Rosa to Alice. It takes form as a silver luminescence surrounding the figures in the right half of the canvas. Compared to *Procession*, the vibration is finer, smoother, and openly healing. The artist is giving the regenerative energy to her mother, who at that time is in a hospital and nearing the end of her life. Beginning with *Go Gentle*, and continuing through the next four paintings, May Stevens nurtures and guides her mother into death, giving symmetry to their time together.

Sometimes when describing a key work, an artist or poet will say, "I don't know where it came from" or "I feel like I didn't do it." This is May Stevens' experience with *Fore River*, which followed *Go Gentle*. She began the painting with the intent of "making Rosa's death site into an important painting." Several small studies of the bridge where Rosa's murderers threw her body into the canal were completed, and eventually one was expanded into a large canvas. But the painting stalled out. To get it going again the artist drew from *Go Gentle* and brought in two large figures of Alice, one on each side of the bridge. As she worked on the figures brush strokes of silver came in and gradually began to cover the image of the bridge. As it became vague the painting came more and more to life. "Like a miracle" a shaft of luminescent energy developed on its own, taking the place of the death site.

The completed painting is hallucinatory and immeasurable. The two Alices, now strangely androgynous, pulsate with anger. A lifetime of pent-up emotion is streaming out of her. The shaft of silver energy, a gift from Rosa, empowers her streaming process, clearing her, readying her for death and for the life to come. The artist has received the gift, she has become a tuned instrument gathering energy from Rosa, transmitting it to Alice. Linear time has lost its hold. *Fore River* is disturbing yet inspiring, destabilizing yet somehow healing. "The key to the riddle is simply life itself, this deep darkness of night is soft and beautiful as velvet, if one only looks at it in the right way."

Winter 1987
Copyright 1987 by Reese Williams

# ENDNOTES

[1]Lewis Hyde, *The Gift* (New York: Random House, 1983); see Chapter 3, "The Labor of Gratitude," more specifically pp. 50-51.

[2]Eliade, *The Myth of the Eternal Return* (Princeton, New Jersey: Princeton University Press, Bollingen Series XLVI, 1971). The entire book is relevant, but specifically Chapter 3, "Misfortune and History."

[3]Luxemburg, *Prison Letters* (London: Square One Pamphlets, Independent Labor Party, 1972), 22, 29.

[4]Luxemburg, *Selected Political Writings* (New York: Grove Press, 1974), edited and introduced by Robert Looker: 306. Luxemburg was referring to the abortive socialist revolution when she wrote in January 1919 in *Die Rote Fahne*, organ of the newly formed German Communist Party: "Tomorrow the revolution will rear its head once again, and to your horror, will proclaim with trumpets blazing: I was, I am, I will be!"

# EXISTENTIAL POEM

May Stevens

There was a child who loved her own breathing
climbed each wave                  teetered on top
eyes lit          toes extended         hands holding on
transfixed in terror         small as she was
not believing          the breath that was
already leaving          was hers
to keep

She killed herself out of curiosity
she killed herself for joy
por el gozo
matate, linda

She wakes from her dream
                         his body blocks the bedlamp
—what is that you want really?
She picks up the rips of her dream
                         slips it over her head
wriggles it down where she left it
                         smooths the torn places
slowly

     Now I lay me down to sleep
     I pray the Lord my soul to keep
     If I should die before I wake
     I pray the Lord my soul to take

She wanted to see her friends
the ones she had loved and the ones
she hadn't met. She wanted to tell them
about the joy

—what do you feel when I take you,
   do what I want with you?

She remembers the leaping moons, the constellations
dropped behind the hill; moments of joining,
clear passage; the feeling of not knowing
what she needed to know; how the feeling
of knowing came at last, like moisture

     The gap closes between breath and breath

A woman within or in juxtaposition to a patriarchal system; in the first case, left-wing politics; in the second, the military. In *The Second International* Rosa Luxemburg penetrates the unity and sameness of the world leaders of socialism in the 1904 Congress in Amsterdam. In *Eden Hotel* the waitress serves the wine to the killers of Rosa Luxemburg who celebrate the day following the murder January 16, 1919. Presence. Absence. Substitution. Proportion. Quota. Power. Powerlessness. One less. One more or less. Rosa Luxemburg flared across the European dark like a meteor, an aberration. Her murder restores the usual dark. The waitress brings her tray. The usual faces look out. Order is restored. In Berlin. In Chile. In El Salvador.

*One Plus or Minus One*, an installation at the New Museum of Contemporary Art, New York City, February 19–April 3, 1988, consisting of three texts and two photomurals, each approximately 11 × 17".

The Congress of the Second International in Amsterdam in 1904 with
thirty-three-year-old Rosa Luxemburg attending as delegate from
Germany and Poland. She is surrounded by the leading figures of
world socialism, including August Bebel and Karl Kautsky, also from
Germany; Jean Jaurès, France; Sen Katayama, Japan; Georgi
Plekhanov, Russia; Keir Hardie, England; Morris Hillquit, U.S.A.
When the great French socialist leader Jaurès attacks Rosa
Luxemburg and the German delegation for, among other things,
continuing to support Dreyfus, there is no one present to translate his
fiery speech from the French. Rosa Luxemburg adds to her triumph
by spontaneously reproducing his polemic against her into equally
vigorous German.

In 1914 at the outbreak of the First World War, Rosa Luxemburg is
convicted of anti-war activities, having urged German workers to
resist the war, to refuse to kill workers from other countries. She
spends the duration of the war in prison, sending out a continuous
flow of letters, articles, and plans for the development of international
socialism. She writes:

> The present World War, whether it brings victory or defeat for
> anyone . . . means the defeat of socialism and democracy . . .
> Today's World War is thus developing all the preconditions for
> new wars.

Released from prison after three years and four months, she returns to
Berlin where she is murdered by a death squad serving as an
unofficial arm of the military.

*The Second International*, 1988.

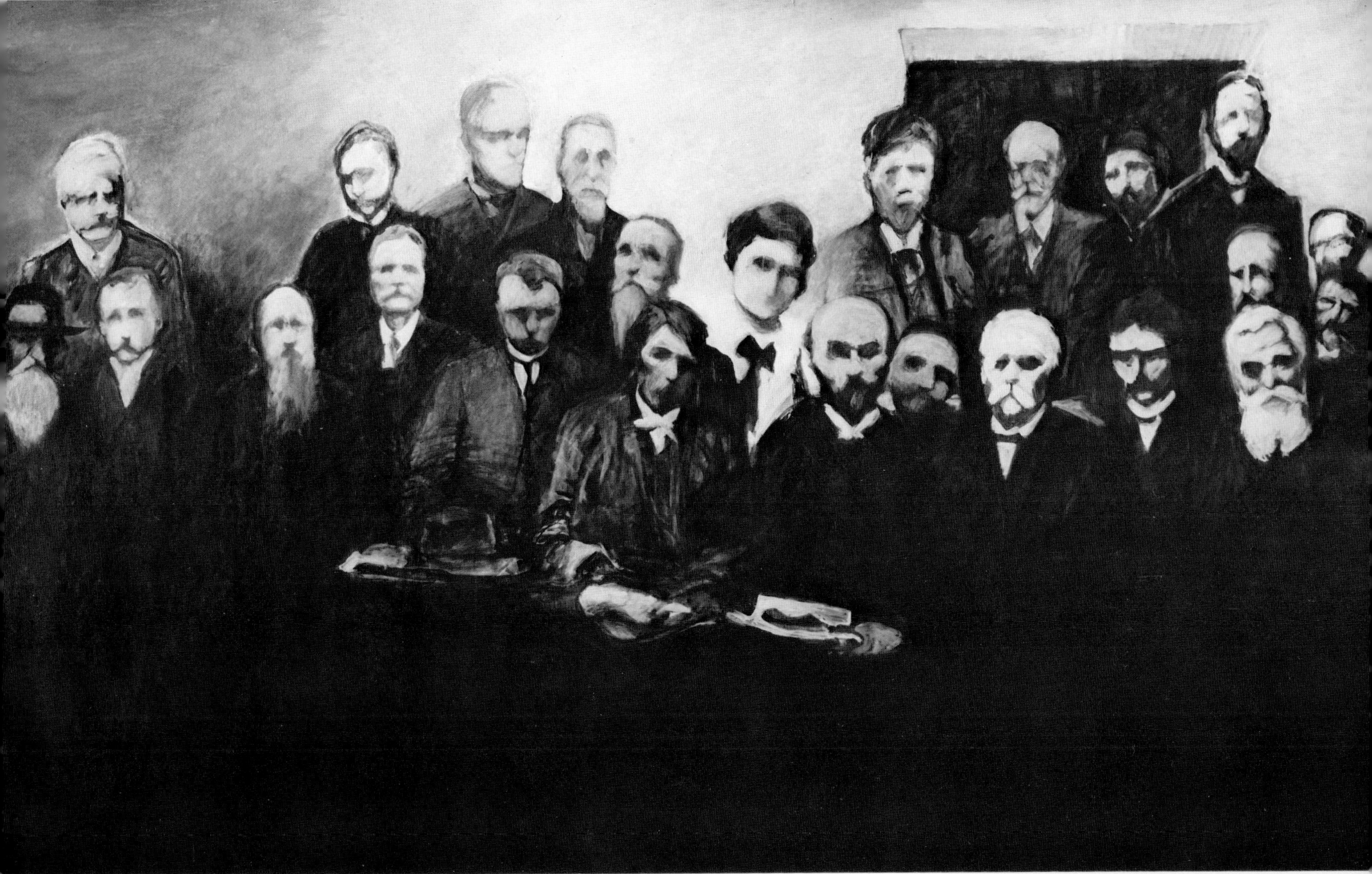

A celebration by soldiers and officers of the Garde-Kavallerie-
Schützen-Division (Division of Cavalry and Riflemen) in their
temporary military headquarters at the Eden Hotel in Berlin on
January 15, 1919, the day following the assassination of Rosa
Luxemburg and Karl Liebknecht.

Rifleman Otto Runge, who administered the two rifle-butt blows to
the head that killed Rosa Luxemburg, and First Lieutenant Vogel,
officer-in-charge, who finished her off with a revolver shot and
ordered her body thrown into the Landwehr Canal, were brought
before a military tribunal May 8–14.

Soldier Runge was sentenced to two years imprisonment for
attempted manslaughter. In 1933 he applied for financial compen-
sation for unjust punishment, citing his early contribution to the Nazi
cause. The government of Adolf Hitler awarded him 6,000
deutschmarks.

First Lieutenant Vogel was convicted of committing a misdemeanor
while on guard duty, of illegally disposing of a corpse, and of filing an
incorrect report. He was sentenced to two years and four months.
However, provided with false passport and visa, he escaped to
Holland the day after sentencing. There he awaited the inevitable
amnesty.

On January 25, 1919, a symbolic funeral took place in the streets of
Berlin; Rosa Luxemburg's coffin was empty. Her body floated to the
surface of the canal on May 31.


*Eden Hotel*, 1988.

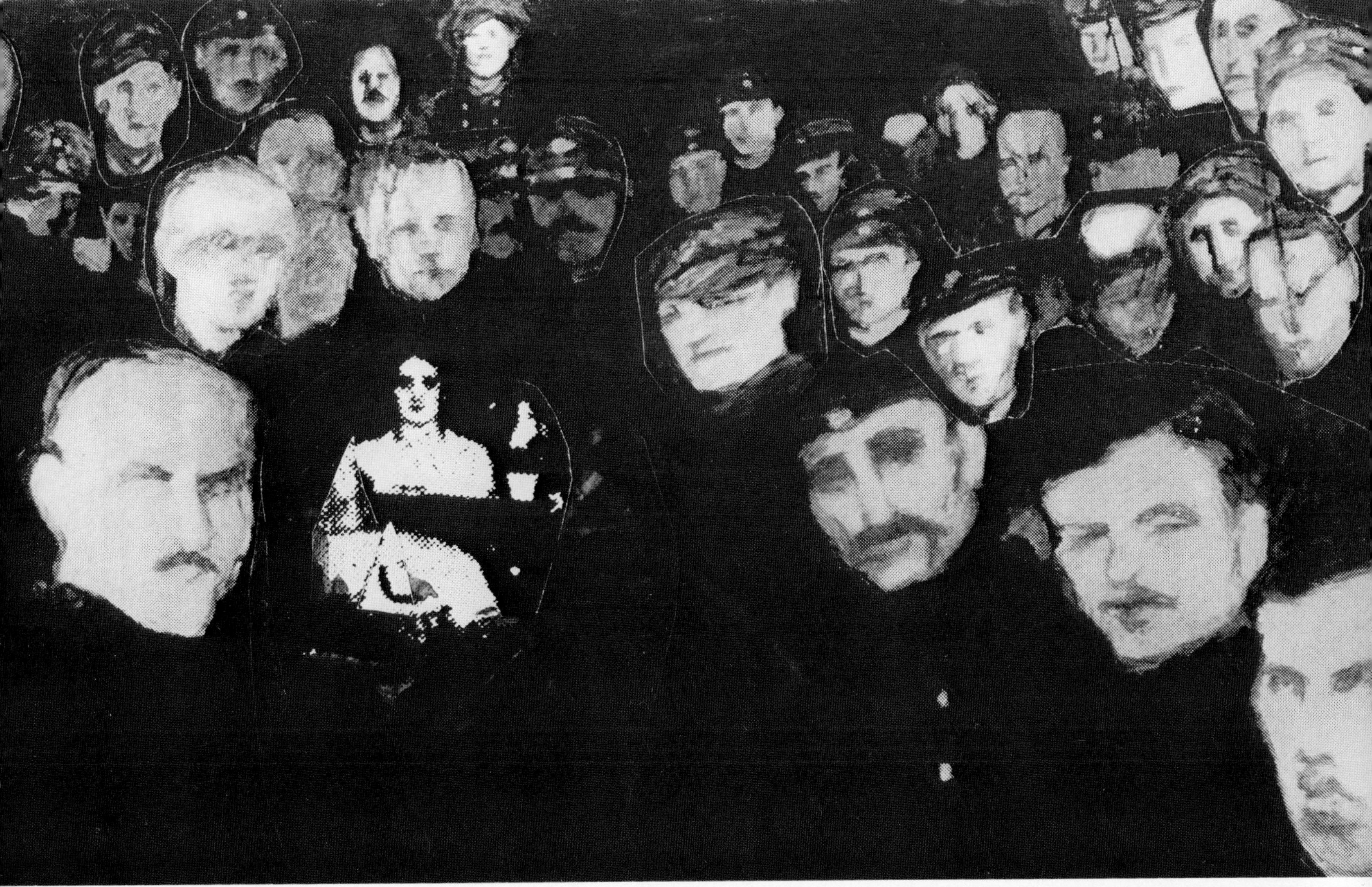

# WORKS IN THE EXHIBITION

(All works are in the collection of the artist unless otherwise noted.)

*Voices*, 1983, acrylic/canvas, 79 × 118″

*The Murderers of Rosa Luxemburg*, 1986, acrylic/canvas, 78 × 129″

*Rosa Luxemburg Attends the Second International*, 1987, acrylic/canvas, 79 × 128″

*A Life*, 1984, acrylic/canvas, 78 × 120″

*Signs*, 1985, acrylic/canvas, 77.5 × 117″

*Dreams and Theories I*, 1981, acrylic/canvas, 48 × 32″

*Dreams and Theories II*, 1981, acrylic/canvas, 48 × 32″, Coll: Elizabeth Hess and Peter Biskind

*Two Women*, 1976, mixed-media collage, 10.5 × 13.5″, Coll: Rudolf Baranik

*Tribute to Rosa Luxemburg*, 1976, mixed-media collage, 16.5 × 10″, Coll: Rudolf Baranik

*Rosa and Alice*, 1977, mixed-media collage, 22 × 17″, Coll: Patricia Hills

*Roza*, 1980, mixed-media collage, 42 × 52″

*Everybody Knows Me*, 1981, mixed media, three panels on foamboard, 60 × 40″ each, Coll: The New Museum of Contemporary Art, New York (gift of the artist).

# BIBLIOGRAPHY AND NOTES

## ARTICLES AND REVIEWS

Alloway, Lawrence. "Essay." In *May Stevens*, exhibition catalogue. Herbert F. Johnson Museum, Cornell University, 1973.

__________. "Art." *The Nation* (February 1976).

__________. "Women's Art in the 70s." *Art in America* (March 1976).

Bonshek, Anna. "Museum of Women." *Artists Newsletter* (September 1986).

Brenson, Michael. "Art: A View of News Manipulation." *New York Times* (March 22, 1986).

Cooper, Emmanuel. "Extending Visual Art Boundaries." *Morning Star* [London] (December 5, 1980).

Cork, Richard. "Now It's the Turn of the Painted Male." *The New Standard* (November 27, 1980).

Evett, Kenneth. "Back to the WPA." *The New Republic* (November 24, 1973).

Glueck, Grace. "Women Artists '80." *Art News* (October 1980).

__________. "May Stevens." *New York Times* (March 20, 1981).

__________. "Art People." *New York Times* (April 24, 1981).

Gouma-Peterson, Thalia and Patricia Mathews. "The Feminist Critique of Art History." *Art Bulletin* (September 1987).

Greyson, John. "Women Artists' Books." *Fuse* (May–June 1981).

Heartney, Eleanor. "May Stevens." *New Art Examiner* (April 1985).

Hess, Elizabeth. "Success! A Boone for Feminists?" *Village Voice* Fall Art Supplement (October 6, 1987).

Kilstedt, Folke T. "Narrowing the Gap: An Interpretation of Recent Works by May Stevens." In *Mysteries and Politics*, exhibition catalogue. Franklin and Marshall College, Lancaster, Pennsylvania, 1979.

King, Martin Luther. Preface in *Freedom Riders*, exhibition catalogue. Roko Gallery, New York City, 1963.

Kingsley, April. "Visions and Revisions." *Village Voice* (January 15, 1979).

Knight, Christopher. "She Paints of Politics and Power." *Los Angeles Herald Examiner* (April 21, 1985).

Kramer, Hilton. "May Stevens." *New York Times* (March 22, 1975).

Kuspit, Donald. "May Stevens at Lerner-Heller." *Art in America* (March 1978).

__________. "Art of Conscience: the Last Decade." *Dialogue* (October–November 1980).

__________. "Art Couples 1: Rudolf Baranik and May Stevens." In *Art Couples 1*, exhibition catalogue. P.S. 1, New York City, October 1982.

__________. "May Stevens Within the Self's Heroic and Unheroic Past." In *Ordinary • Extraordinary, A Summation*, exhibition catalogue. Boston University Art Gallery, March 1984, and Frederick S. Wight Gallery, University of California at Los Angeles, April 1985.

Larson, Kay. "May Stevens." *Art News* (January 1979).

__________. "May Stevens." *New York Magazine* (March 23, 1981).

Liebman, Lisa. "May Stevens at Lerner-Heller." *Art in America*

(November 1981).

Linker, Kate. "Out of the Galleries, Into the Books." *Seven Days* (October 3, 1978).

Lippard, Lucy. "Caring: Five Political Artists." *Studio International* (March 1977).

————. "Issue and Tabu." In *Issue*, exhibition catalogue. Institute of Contemporary Art, London, 1980.

————. "Masses and Meetings." In *Ordinary • Extraordinary, A Summation*, exhibition catalogue. Boston University Art Gallery, March 1984, and Frederick S. Wight Gallery, University of California at Los Angeles, April 1985.

Lister, Ardele. "Edge Junction: Words in Art." *Criteria* 4, no. 1 (Spring 1978).

Marmer, Nancy. "Art and Politics." *Art in America* (July–August 1977).

Mathews, Patricia. "A Dialogue of Silence: May Stevens' Ordinary/ Extraordinary, 1977–86." *Art Criticism* 3, no. 2 (Summer 1987).

Moore, Alan. "May Stevens." *Artforum* (Summer 1977).

Morowski, Stefan. "Neofeminizm w Sztuce." *Sztuca* (1976).

Morreau, Jacqueline. "Review: Visual Arts." *Women's Review* 13 (1986).

Muchnic, Suzanne. "From a Riot of Quilts to a Stilled Life." *Los Angeles Times* (May 9, 1985).

Neugroschel, Joachim. "May Stevens." *Artforum* (December 1971).

Nochlin, Linda. "Some Women Realists: Part 1." *Arts* (February 1974).

Parada, Esther. "Women's Vision Extends the Map of Memory." *Michigan Quarterly Review* (Winter 1987).

Phillips, Deborah. "Definitely Not for Framing." *Art News* (December 1981).

Pollock, Griselda. "The Politics of Art or an Aesthetic for Women." *FAN* 5 (1982).

Richards, Margaret. "Social Exposures." *Tribune* [London] (December 5, 1980).

Roth, Moira. "Visions and Revisions, Rosa Luxemburg and the Artist's Mother." *Artforum* (November 1980).

Schwartz, Therese. "The Politicalization of the Avant-Garde." *Art in America* (November–December 1971).

Scott, Joanna. "Parting Glances." *Afterimage* 14, no. 10 (May 1987).

Stapen, Nancy. "Old Whine in New Bottles." *Art New England* (February 1987).

Steyn, Juliet. "The Other America, an Interview with May Stevens." *Fires* (Spring 1987).

Tickner, Lisa. "Ordinary • Extraordinary." *Block 5* (Fall 1981).

Wallach, Alan. "May Stevens: On the Stage of History." *Arts* (November 1978).

Weisberg, Ruth. "Two Women Juxtaposed." *Artweek* (May 11, 1985).

Withers, Josephine. "Re-visioning our Foremothers: Reflections on the Ordinary/Extraordinary Art of May Stevens." *Feminist Studies* 13, no. 3 (Fall 1987).

Wooster, Ann-Sargent. "May Stevens." *Art News* (December 1976.)

Zimmer, William. "Ten Major Women Artists." *New York Times* (March 22, 1987).

# BOOKS

Ashton, Dore. *American Art Since 1945*. New York: Oxford University Press, 1982.

Battcock, Gregory. *Superrealism*. New York: E.P. Dutton, 1975.

Cox, Sue. *Female Psychology: The Emerging Self*. Chicago, Toronto, Paris: Science Research Associates, 1976.

Hammond, Harmony. *Wrappings*. New York: TSL Press, 1984.

Howe, Irwing. *Images of Labor*. Princeton, New Jersey: Pilgrim Press, 1981.

Lippard, Lucy. *From the Center*. New York: E.P. Dutton, 1976.

Lippard, Lucy. *Get the Message?* New York: E.P. Dutton, 1984.

Loeb, Judy. *Feminist Collage*. New York: Columbia University Teachers College Press, 1979.

Lucie-Smith, Edward. *Art in the Seventies*. Ithaca, New York: Cornell University Press, 1980.

Miller, Lynn F. and Sally Swenson. *Lives and Works*. Metuchen, New

Jersey: The Scarecrow Press, 1981.

Munro, Eleanor. *Originals: American Women Artists*. New York: Simon and Schuster, 1979.

*National Museum of Women in the Arts* (catalogue of the collection). New York: Harry N. Abrams, 1987.

Naylor, Colin. *Contemporary Artists*. London: St. James Press; New York: St. Martin's Press, 1977.

Parker, Rosika and Griselda Pollock, eds. *Framing Feminism: Art and the Women's Movement 1970–85*. London: Pandora, 1987.

Robinson, Hilary, ed. *Visibly Female: Feminism and Art Today, an Anthology*. London: Camden Press, 1987.

Rubinstein, Charlotte Streifer. *American Women Artists*. New York: Avon Publishers, 1982.

Sandel, Renee and Georgia Collins. *Women, Art, and Education*. Reston, Virginia: National Art Education Association, 1984.

Schwartz, Barry. *The New Humanism: Art in a Time of Change*. New York and Washington: Praeger Publishers, 1974.

Selz, Peter. *Art in Our Times: A Pictorial History, 1890–1980*. New York: Abrams Publishers, 1981.

Stich, Sidra. *Made in U.S.A., An Americanization in Modern Art, the '50s and the '60s*. Berkeley: University of California Press, 1987.

Walker, John A. *Rosa Luxemburg and Karl Liebnecht: Revolution, Remembrance, Representation*. London: Pentonville Gallery, 1986.


# WRITINGS BY MAY STEVENS

"Painters Reply." *Artforum* (September 1975).

"Art and Class." *The Fox* 3 (1976).

"My Work and My Working-Class Father." In *Working It Out*, edited by Sara Ruddick and Pamela Daniels. New York: Pantheon Books, 1977.

"*Eva Hesse* by Lucy Lippard." *Women Artists Newsletter* (1977).

"Radical Art: Theory and Practice." Proceedings of the "Marxism and Art" caucus. Los Angeles: College Art Association, January 1978.

"May Stevens on Jane Cooper on Rosa Luxemburg." In *Voices of Women: 3 on 3 on 3*, edited by Cynthia Navaretta. New York: Midmarch Associates, 1980.

"Taking Art to the Revolution." *Heresies* 9 (1980).

"Class." *Conditions: Six* 2, no. 3 (Summer 1980).

"Ordinary Extraordinary." In *Between Women*, edited by Carol Asher, Louise DiSalvo, and Sara Ruddick. Boston: Beacon Press, 1984.


# EXHIBITIONS

**1988**

Special Project, Orchard Gallery, Derry, Northern Ireland.

*One Plus or Minus One*, special project, New Museum of Contemporary Art, New York City.

*Committed to Print*, 1960 to present, Museum of Modern Art, New York City.

*Rosa Alice, May Stevens' Ordinary Extraordinary*, Kenyon College, Gambier, Ohio.

*New Works From Ordinary Extraordinary*, Real Art Ways, Hartford, Connecticut.

*Vietnam and Artists' Perspectives*, San Jose Museum, California.

*The Social Club*, Exit Art, New York City.


**1987**

*Artists' Mothers: Portraits and Homages*, Heckscher Museum, Huntington, New York.

*Made in U.S.A.: Art from the '50s and '60s*, University Museum, Berkeley, California.

*Concrete Crisis: Urban Images of the '80s*, Exit Art, New York City.

*Connections Project/Conexus*, Museum of Contemporary Hispanic Art, New York City.

*Images of Power*, Rockland Center for the Arts, New York.

*Women's Autobiographical Artists' Book*, University of Wisconsin, Milwaukee, Wisconsin.

### 1986
*Rosa Luxemburg and Karl Liebknecht: Revolution, Remembrance, Representation*, Pentonville Gallery, London.
*The Law and Order Show*, Barbara Gladstone Gallery, New York City.
*Feminist Photo-Graphics*, Hunter College, New York City.
*Art in the Community—Community Art?*, Maidstone College of Art, London.
*Letters*, The Clocktower, New York City.
*Homage to Ana Mendieta*, Zeus Trabia Gallery, New York City.
*Por Encima del Bloqueo*, Casa de la Obra Pia, Havana, Cuba.
*En Camino a Cuba*, Museo Universitario del Chopo, Mexico City.

### 1985
*The Other America*, Royal Festival Hall, London.
*Photo-Synthesis*, One Penn Plaza, New York City.
*Adornments*, Bernice Steinbaum Gallery, New York City.
*Latitudes of Time*, City Gallery, New York City.
*American Women in Art: Works on Paper*, United Nations International Conference on Women, Nairobi, Kenya.

### 1984
*Ordinary • Extraordinary, A Summation 1977–84*, Boston University Art Gallery, Boston, Massachusetts.
*Tradition and Conflict, 1963–1973*, The Studio Museum in Harlem, New York City.
*1 + 1 = 2*, Bernice Steinbaum Gallery, New York City, and Boca Raton Museum, Boca Raton, Florida.

### 1983
*Exchange of Sources: Expanding Powers*, California State College at Stanislaus, Turlock, California.
*Portraits on a Human Scale*, Whitney Museum (Downtown Branch), New York City.

*Issues and Images*, Emerson Gallery, Hamilton College, Clinton, New York.

### 1982
*Text/Picture Notes*, Visual Studies Workshop, Rochester, New York.
*Indiana-New York Connection*, Snite Museum of Art, University of Notre Dame, Indiana.
*4 Art and Photography Portfolios*, City Gallery, New York City.
*Beyond Aesthetics*, Henry Street Settlement House, New York City.
*Ordinary Extraordinary*, Clark University, Worcester, Massachusetts.
*Window Work*, Mason Gross School of the Arts, Rutgers University, New Brunswick, New Jersey.
*Sense and Sensibility*, Midland Group, Nottingham, England.
*Art Couples 1: May Stevens and Rudolf Baranik*, P.S. 1, New York City.

### 1981
*Ikon/Logos. Word as Image*, Alternative Museum, New York City.
*Window Work*, Printed Matter, New York City.
*The Page as Alternative Space*, Franklin Furnace, New York City.
*Artists by Artists*, Whitney Museum (Downtown Branch), New York City.
*Images of Labor*, District 1199 Headquarters, New York City (circulated by the Smithsonian Institution).

### 1980
*Issue: Social Strategies by Women Artists*, Institute of Contemporary Art, London.
*Art of Conscience: The Last Decade*, Wright State University, Dayton, Ohio (circulated by the Ohio State Council on the Arts).
*International Feminist Art*, Gemeentemuseum, The Hague, Netherlands.
*Political Commentary in Contemporary Art*, State University of New York at Potsdam and State University of New York at Binghamton.

### 1979
*Artists By Artists*, Whitney Museum (Downtown Branch), New York City.
*Mysteries and Politics*, Franklin and Marshall College, Lancaster,

Pennsylvania.
*Rosa Luxemburg Series*, C Space, New York City, and Texas Tech University, Lubbock, Texas.
*Drawing Invitational*, Western Carolina University, Cullowhee, North Carolina, and University of Mississippi, University, Mississippi.

**1978**
*Three History Paintings*, Lerner-Heller Gallery, New York City.
*Painting and Sculpture Today*, Indianapolis Museum of Art, Indianapolis, Indiana.
*New York Now*, Wordworks, San Jose, California.
*Master Drawings*, University Art Gallery, Creighton University, Omaha, Nebraska.

**1977**
*Dotty Attie/May Stevens Drawings*, Manhattanville College, Purchase, New York.
*Strong Works* (including Bartlett, Kosloff, Morton, Steir), Artemisia Gallery, Chicago, Illinois.
*May Stevens*, Pelham von Stoffler Gallery, Houston, Texas.
*Consciousness and Content*, Brooklyn Museum, New York City.
*Ten Years Ten Downtown*, P.S. 1, New York City.
*Ten Years Ten Downtown Documentation*, 112 Greene Street, New York City.

**1976**
*The American Flag in the Art of Our Country*, Allentown Art Museum, Allentown, Pennsylvania.
*A Patriotic Show*, Lerner-Heller Gallery, New York City; Wright State University, Dayton, Ohio; University of Connecticut, Storrs, Connecticut.
*An American Symbol*, Minneapolis Institute of Art, Minneapolis, Minnesota.
*May Stevens/New Realist Work*, Lerner-Heller Gallery, New York City.
*Color, Light, and Image*, Women's Interart Center, New York City.

*Three American Realists: Neel, Sleigh, Stevens*, Everson Museum, Syracuse, New York.
*Drawings and Poems*, Queens College, New York City.

**1975**
*May Stevens: Selections Big Daddy 1968–75*, Lerner-Heller Gallery, New York City.
*May Stevens*, Deson-Zaks Gallery, Chicago, Illinois.
*Sons and Others: Women Artists See Men*, Queens Museum, New York City.
*Paintings Eligible for Purchase under the Childe Hassam Fund* (purchase), American Academy of Arts and Letters, New York City.
*May Stevens, Recent Paintings*, University of Wisconsin, Menomonie, Wisconsin.

**1974**
*May Stevens: Women Artists Series Year 4*, Douglass College, New Brunswick, New Jersey.
*Watergate, Speglat AV Americanska Konstnarer*, Galerie Borjeson, Malmo, Sweden.
*May Stevens*, Soho 20, New York City.
*May Stevens*, Bienville Gallery, New Orleans, Louisiana.

**1973**
*May Stevens*, Herbert F. Johnson Museum, Cornell University, Ithaca, New York.
*Women Choose Women*, New York Cultural Center, New York City.
*Drawings 1973*, Minnesota Museum of Art, St. Paul, Minnesota.
*Voices of Alarm*, Lerner-Heller Gallery, New York City; Moravian College, Bethlehem, Pennsylvania.

**1972**
*American Women Artists Show, Gedok*, Kunsthaus, Hamburg, West Germany.
*Eighteenth National Print Exhibition*, Brooklyn Museum, New York City.

**1971**
*The Permanent Collection: Women Artists*, Whitney Museum, New York City.
*May Stevens*, Terry Dintenfass Gallery, New York City.
*Collage of Indignation II*, New York Cultural Center and Hundred Acres Gallery, New York City.

**1970**
*Ten Downtown Loft Exhibition*, New York City.
*Paintings Eligible for Purchase under the Childe Hassam Fund* (purchase), American Academy of Arts and Letters, New York City.

**1969**
*Paintings Eligible for Purchase under the Childe Hassam Fund* (purchase), American Academy of Arts and Letters, New York City, New York.

**1968**
*May Stevens*, Roko Gallery, New York City.

**1967**
*Collage of Indignation*, Loeb Student Center, New York University, New York City.

**1966**
*Landscapes*, Visual Arts Gallery, New York City.
*The Peace Tower*, Los Angeles, California.
*New York '66*, Hampton Institute, Hampton, Virginia.

**1965**
*65 Self-Portraits*, Visual Arts Gallery, New York City.

**1964**
*159th Annual Exhibition*, Pennsylvania Academy, Philadelphia, Pennsylvania.

*Exhibition of Paintings*, The National Institute of Arts and Letters, New York City.

**1963**
*Freedom Riders (Paintings by May Stevens)*, Roko Gallery, New York City.

**1962**
*Commemoration of 65th Birthday of Siqueiros*, ACA Gallery, New York City.

**1961**
*May Stevens*, Roland de Anelle Gallery, New York City.
*The Figure Then and Now*, Roland de Anelle Gallery, New York City.

**1959**
*24th Annual Midyear Show*, Butler Institute of American Art, Youngstown, Ohio.

**1958**
*Ninth Annual New England Exhibition*, Silvermine Guild, Connecticut.

**1957**
*May Stevens*, ACA Gallery, New York City.

**1955**
*May Stevens*, Galerie Moderne, New York City.

**1951**
*May Stevens*, Galerie Huit, Paris.
*Salon De Jeunes Peintres*, Paris.
*Salon D'Automne*, Paris.
*Salon De Femmes Peintres*, Paris.

# AWARDS

National Institute of Arts and Letters Purchase Award, 1968, 1969, 1975
MacDowell Art Colony Fellowship, 1971, 1972, 1974, 1975, 1977, 1981, 1982, 1984, 1985, 1987
New York State Council on the Arts Creative Artists Public Service Award in graphics, 1974
LINE Association Grant for artists' book, 1978
National Endowment for the Arts Grant in painting, 1983
Guggenheim Fellowship in painting, 1986

# PUBLIC COLLECTIONS

Whitney Museum of American Art, San Francisco Museum of Modern Art, Herbert F. Johnson Museum of Cornell University, Everson Museum, Allentown Museum of Art, Brooklyn Museum, University of Wisconsin at Menomonie, Nassau Museum of Art, Queens Museum, Ball State University Museum, Dulin Gallery of Art, Hampton Institute Museum, Jacksonville Art Museum, Schenectady Museum, Ohio State University Collection, School of Visual Arts, University of Miami, Wichita State University Museum, Washington University in St. Louis.

# BIOGRAPHICAL NOTE

May Stevens was born in Boston, Massachusetts, in 1924. She studied at the Massachusetts College of Art (earning a B.F.A. in 1946), the Art Students League in New York City, and the Academie Julian in Paris. She lives in New York City and teaches at the School of Visual Arts.

# LENDERS TO THE EXHIBITION

Rudolf Baranik

Elizabeth Hess and Peter Biskind

Patricia Hills

The New Museum of Contemporary Art, New York City

# KEY TO FIGURES